Unraveling Our Story through God's Covenants

threaded

BIBLE STUDY GUIDE + STREAMING VIDEO | SIX SESSIONS

TARA BETH LEACH

HarperChristian Resources

Threaded Bible Study Guide

Published in Grand Rapids, Michigan, by HarperChristian Resources. HarperChristian Resources is a registered trademark of HarperCollins Christian Publishing, Inc.

Requests for information should be sent to customercare@harpercollins.com.

ISBN 978-0-310-17193-5 (softcover)

ISBN 978-0-310-17194-2 (ebook)

HarperChristian Resources titles may be purchased in bulk for church, business, fundraising, or ministry use. For information, please e-mail ResourceSpecialist@ChurchSource.com.

First Printing March 2025 / Printed in the United States of America

contents

introduction

Welcome to the journey of discovering the beautiful, intricate threads of God's story—a story that has been woven together with divine intention from the beginning. This is not a haphazard tapestry; it is one designed by the hands of a loving Creator who has always had a plan. You see, every thread tells a part of the story, connecting what was to what is and what will be. And at the center of this story is a God who is not distant but who has leaned into the brokenness, into the chaos, and into our lives to bring about redemption.

From the first breath of creation, when God's Spirit hovered over the waters (Genesis 1:2), there was a plan. The fabric of the universe was laced with *shalom*—wholeness, peace, and harmony. Everything fit together perfectly. Humanity walked with God in communion with Him, with each other, and with the world around them. But something unraveled. The moment humanity pulled away from God's design, the thread of sin began to fray the beautiful tapestry. Chaos crept in, and things fell apart. But friends, here's the truth: God didn't fall apart. His plan remained intact. His love didn't waver.

The story of God is one of *holy mending,* of gathering the loose and broken threads and weaving them back into something even more beautiful than before. It's a story of covenants—promises made by a faithful God to His people. These covenants are not random or disconnected but are part of a single thread that runs through the entirety of Scripture, binding everything together. The covenants are God's way of saying, "I'm not finished yet. I'm still weaving."

The Noahic Covenant, the Abrahamic Covenant, the Mosaic Covenant, the Davidic Covenant—all of these are promises that build toward the ultimate fulfillment of these promises in Jesus Christ. Each covenant reveals more of God's character, His faithfulness, and His unrelenting desire to restore the world to its intended beauty. And here's the good news: we are a part of that story. We are invited into this divine tapestry and called to see our lives as part of something much larger than ourselves—a plan that has always existed and is still unfolding today.

In this study, we will learn about and lean into these sacred threads. We'll explore how each covenant is not just a historical moment but also a living invitation for us to trust God more deeply, to see His redemptive hand in our lives, and to become participants in His ongoing work of restoration. You may find yourself resonating with Noah, who was asked to trust God's plan in the midst of chaos, or with Abraham, who had to leave behind all that was familiar to him to follow God into the unknown. Wherever you find yourself in the story, know this: there is a place for you in God's grand narrative.

As we move through each week, I encourage you to approach this study with an open heart. This is not just about learning biblical facts but is also about transformation. It's about being shaped by the promises of God and letting those promises guide how we live, how we love, and how we serve. The covenants of the Bible remind us that God has not abandoned His creation—far from it. He is still working, still weaving, still drawing us into the beauty of His plan. And as we lean into these promises, we will discover that, though the world is often frayed and chaotic, God's faithfulness is our anchor. His covenantal love is our thread of hope, holding us fast.

So, as we embark on this journey together, may you feel the tug of these divine threads in your life. May you see how God has always been weaving your story into His, and may you be reminded that this grand tapestry is not yet finished. There is more beauty to come.

Let's lean in, together.

Your Journey Partner,

Tara Beth Leach

the structure of the study

This study is divided into **six weeks,** and each week will invite you into a deeper reflection on the nature of God's promises through the covenants He made. There are also six video sessions, which will guide the discussion for each group session, providing rich teaching and insight into the week's theme. You'll find that the covenants we will explore—Noahic, Abrahamic, Mosaic, Davidic—all point to the new covenant of Jesus, which represents the ultimate fulfillment of God's redemptive plan.

Each week, you will have four days of personal Bible study, which include time for you to **read**, **study**, **reflect**, and **pray**. On **Day 5 of each week**, you will be guided through the practice of **contemplative prayer**—a space where you can quiet your heart, still your mind, and enter into a deep and reflective experience of God's presence. This fifth day is crucial in that it gives you room not just to learn but to *be*.

Contemplative prayer, as practiced by the early church, is a way of resting in God's presence without the need for words or even petitions. As Augustine once wrote, "You have made us for yourself, O Lord, and our heart is restless until it rests in you" (*Confessions* 1.1).[1] Contemplative prayer represents an invitation to rest in the Lord, to find your place in His story, and to be reminded that the God who made you is weaving your life into something beautiful.

Contemplative prayer is not about producing something or achieving a particular spiritual state. Instead, it is about **resting in the love of God**, trusting that even in the silence He is at work. As St. John of the Cross reminds us, "The soul that is quick to turn to speaking and conversing with God is slow to be a listener. God speaks in the silence of the heart, and we must learn to listen."[2] On these days, you will be guided into this silence, into this holy listening, trusting that God is present even in the stillness.

---

1 Augustine. *Confessions*. Translated by Henry Chadwick, Oxford University Press, 1991, Book I, Chapter 1, p. 3.

2 Kieran Kavanaugh and Otilio Rodriguez, trans., *The Collected Works of St. John of the Cross, rev. ed. (Washington, DC: Institute of Carmelite Studies, 1991), 164.*

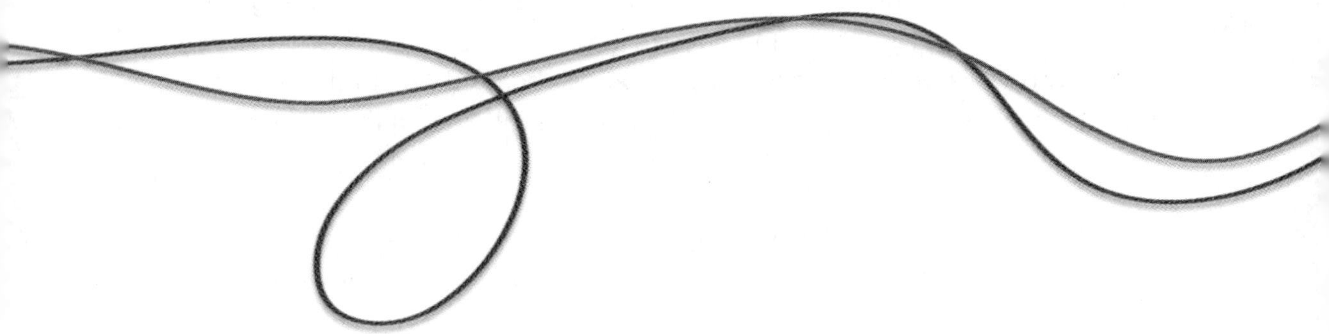

how to use this study guide

This study is designed to help you encounter God's redemptive story through the covenants. Here's a guide for how to make the most of your time:

1. **Group Sessions:** Each week, you'll gather with your group to watch one of the six video sessions that correspond with the covenants. These videos will help set the stage for your week's study and provide a foundation for group discussion. Make sure to engage with the group questions after the video, and don't be afraid to share your reflections and insights. You can watch the videos on your own or as a group. The streaming instructions for the videos can be found in the front cover of this study guide.

2. **Personal Study Days (Days 1–4):** After the group session, you will have four personal study days each week. These days will guide you through this process:

   - **Read:** A passage of Scripture tied to the covenant being studied.
   - **Study:** Thought-provoking questions to help you understand the passage in its context and what it reveals about God's covenantal plan.
   - **Reflect:** This section invites you to consider how the passage and covenant intersect with your own life, prompting a personal response.
   - **Pray:** A prayer guide to help you seek God's wisdom, presence, and guidance as you internalize the truth you've studied.

3. **Day 5—Contemplative Prayer:** Day 5 is intentionally different. It is a day of **prayerful reflection** drawing from the rich tradition of contemplative prayer. This practice allows you to sit with the truths you've studied and offer them back to God, not through more words or actions but through stillness and presence. You are invited to slow down, create space, and listen for the still, small voice of God. As Thomas Merton wrote, *"Contemplation is the highest expression of man's intellectual and spiritual life. It is that life itself, fully awake, fully active, fully aware that it is alive."*[3]

---

3 Thomas Merton, *New Seeds of Contemplation* (New York: New Directions, 1961), 1.

Through these prayer moments, we hope you'll find God speaking to you in ways that deepen your understanding of His covenants and His love for you.

Each lesson is a journey, and we encourage you to go at your own pace, allowing the truths of God's Word to settle deep in your soul. Lean into the mystery, embrace the silence, and let the threads of God's redemptive plan come alive in your heart and mind.

the hard truth of our journey in life

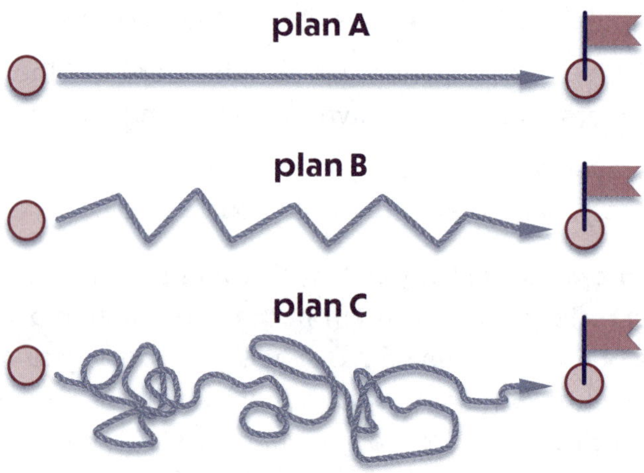

Session 1

The Covenant with Noah

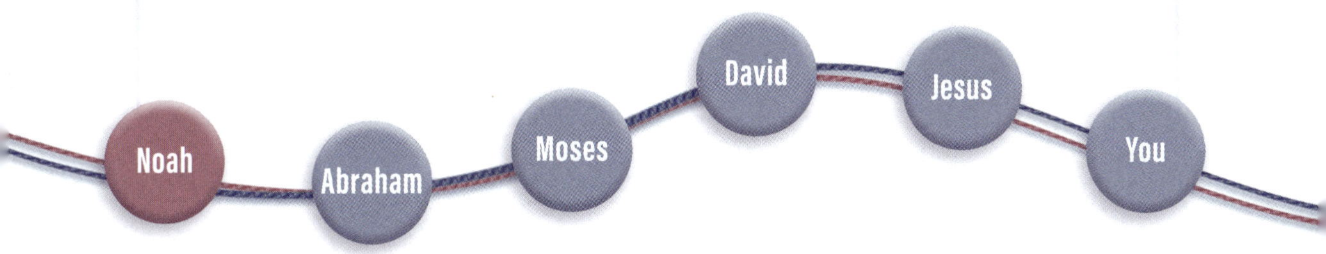

group session (90 minutes)

introduction

Welcome and introductions if the group is new to each other (2 minutes)

Icebreaker and Opening (10 minutes)

Question: *What is the best invitation you've ever received?*

Select a volunteer to read the following aloud to your group:

> The story of God throughout the Bible is not random or accidental—it's the unfolding of a bigger plan that has always been in place. From the beginning, God has been weaving together a story of redemption and healing, inviting humanity to be a part of His work in the world. But it's also a story full of surprises. God often works in ways we don't expect, and it leaves us wondering, *What could God possibly be up to?*
>
> The account of Noah and the flood is one of the first big moments in this plan. It's not just a stand-alone story of a man building an ark. It's part of a much larger promise—a promise that even though humanity had made a mess of things, God wasn't giving up on creation. Through the Noahic Covenant, God begins to set in motion His plan to restore the world. (If you're wondering, Noahic is pronounced like this: Noh-AY-ik).

As we lean into this first video session, let's open our hearts to the unexpected ways God works and how we might be called into His plan of redemption and healing.

prayer

Pray together in unison or select a volunteer to read for your group. Commit yourselves to hearing from the Lord as you go through this study and seek Him continually.

Dearest God of Redemption, we thank You for this opportunity to lean into Your very good and holy word. We thank You that in the beginning, You hovered above the waters, and we believe that same God is present in this space, weaving the threads of past and present together for Your good and glory. Help us to set aside all distraction, pretense, and assumption to come to You with open ears, hearts, and minds. God, we boldly ask that this study would propel us into a holier life, redeemed by the blood of the lamb. We are wholly surrendered to You. Have Your way, Lord. Amen.

read before watching

Ask a volunteer to read Genesis 6 aloud before watching the video.

From the beginning, God had been weaving together a story of redemption and healing, inviting humanity to be a part of His work in the world.

video

watch video session 1 (23:30 minutes)
The Covenant with Noah

Leader, stream the video using access instructions on the inside front cover, or play the DVD (sold separately).

notes

Use this space to take notes from the teaching if you like.

group discussion

(40 minutes)

Leader, read the following prompts to the group for discussion.

Tara Beth unpacked the beginnings of God's redemptive narrative of the Bible and the concept of *shalom*. *Shalom* is the biblical idea that set the scene for God's intentions for creation. Humanity was in right relationship with God, with creation, and with one another. It was humanity that pulled the thread of *shalom* that unleashed sin and brokenness in this world (Genesis 3). God could have abandoned His creation because of humanity's failings. But instead, God pursues.

1. **Think about a time when you experienced grace or mercy when you didn't deserve it. Share that experience with the group.**

The Noahic Covenant was established after the world had become deeply broken, full of violence and evil. In Genesis 6–9 we read about a flood God sent in response to this brokenness. But even in the midst of judgment, God shows mercy by saving Noah and his family, and through His covenant with Noah God promises never to destroy the earth with a flood again. The rainbow becomes a sign of this promise—a reminder that even when things seem dark, God's faithfulness remains.

God's story is a single thread of redemption.

2. **How does understanding the story of creation, *shalom*, and the fall help you grasp the importance of the covenant with Noah?**

The world is full of hurt, division, and death, and it's easy to become disillusioned.

3. **How does the story of Noah and God's promise to never flood the earth again speak to God's character and faithfulness? (See Genesis 9:12–17 for reference.)**

The Bible reveals God's plan to restore the world back to full relationship with Him, which is completed in the story of Jesus.

4. **How does the covenant with Noah set the stage for God's redemptive plan?**

5. **What does the story of Noah teach us about trusting God's promises, both then and now? How does it affect your understanding of His faithfulness?**

In the Noahic Covenant, God gave responsibilities to humanity.

6. **How do those responsibilities shape the way we live as Christians today?**

closing reflection

Leader, read these prompts to the group and provide some time for reflection and response.

- What is one key takeaway from today's discussion that you will carry with you this week?

- How can we pray for each other to grow in our understanding and application of God's covenants?

close in prayer

Read aloud together or select a volunteer to pray over your group.

Dearest Redemptive God, we thank You that You have not left us or forsaken us. Instead, You have leaned in and poured out Your goodness, mercy, and grace. Help us not to let Your good gifts be in vein. Help us receive Your gifts with gratitude for transformation. This week, help us see Your redemptive hand in ordinary moments. May we see the sacred in the mundane and the holy in unexpected places. May we be mediators of Your holiness in Your world in Your way. Amen.

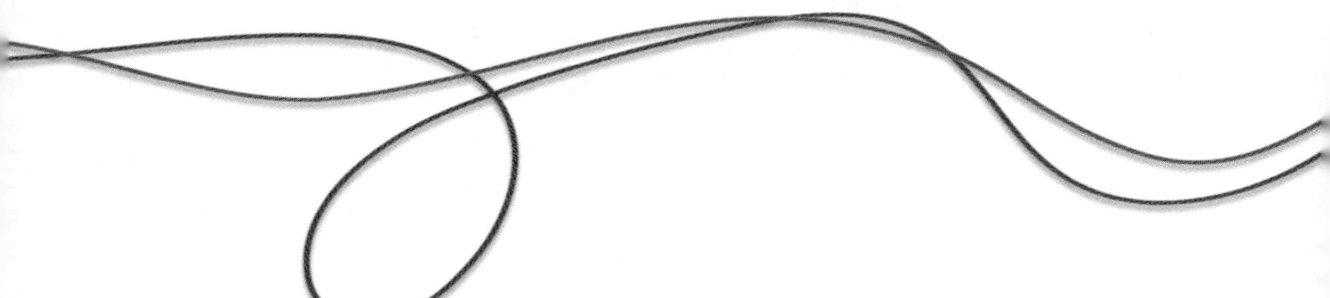

Session 1

personal Bible study

The Covenant with Noah

day 1

Introduction to Covenants and the Story of Noah

Dear one, this is your holy moment. It is yours to claim, to see, to hear, and to experience. Our redemptive God is an experienced reality—He is a God who relates, sees, ministers, and shepherds. Take a deep breath, settle into this holy now. Turn off distractions or notifications on your device if possible. These moments are carved out for you to hear the God who does indeed speak.

Today, as we dig deeper into the Noahic Covenant, let's first remember where the story went awry. What we will discover is God concludes that humanity has abandoned God's vision for shalom. God's vision was quickly and abruptly discarded and forsaken by His beloved creation. This serious problem led to wickedness and evil in the opening verses of Genesis 6. But God's extension of grace that threads through the story is the beginning of our covenant journey together.

read

Genesis 6:1–8

study

What are the reasons given for the flood in Genesis 6:1–8?

What does this passage tell us about the state of humanity at that time?

In Genesis 6:5, it says, "The Lord saw how great the wickedness of the human race had become on the earth." Make a list of what "wickedness" refers to in this context. Consider actions or attitudes that go against God's will.

It is often tempting to evade self-reflection and blame wickedness on other people "out there." But the reality is, "all have sinned" as the apostle Paul reminds us in Romans 3:23. Take a few moments to get honest about the wickedness in your own heart. Confession always leads to forgiveness and grace, as John reminds us in 1 John 1:9. Write a letter of confession to God knowing His whole heart is love and His whole plan is forgiveness for redemption.

pray

In closing, write a prayer of gratitude, embracing the steadfast love and forgiveness of God.

day 2

The Covenant Established

Your holy moment is here yet again, beloved. Don't let these moments slip by you or become routine, but instead remember that God is a relational God, desiring to commune with you as you commune with Him. Yesterday, we read about the dim view of humanity's character. It's a reminder of our incapability of rescuing ourselves, and our need for a redemptive plan. We cannot be saved without the grace and mercy of God, and the Noahic Covenant invites us to remember God's move from judgment to salvation. The story takes an irreversible turn that surprises the reader to imagine what's possible with the promises of God. God remembered His love for His creation. In response to God's goodness, Noah worshiped.

As you settle into today's study, take a few moments to thank God for His remembrance and compassion for His wicked and wayward creation. In your own words, write a prayer to God.

read

Genesis 6:9–22

study

In all the covenants, we will notice a single thread of not only redemption but also an expectation of obedience. Obedience is key to any covenant gifted by God to humanity. A covenant isn't a one-way street of mercy; it is a two-way street of commitment to the framework of the covenant.

When you read Genesis 6:9–22, how does Noah respond to God's instructions in these verses?

____

____

Read the following passages in order and fill in the chart:

Reading	Write out the command.	What was the response?
Genesis 6:21-22		
Genesis 7:1-5		

read

John 12:50

Observe the power of obedience (doing what the Father has told us to do). What does obedience lead to?

What can we learn from Noah's obedience in our own walk with God?

read

Hebrews 11:7

What are examples of faith put into action in Noah's life?

reflect

Reflect on a time when you felt called to obey God in a difficult situation. What was the outcome, and how did it affect your faith?

In what areas of your life do you find it most difficult to trust God? Why do you think that is?

Reflect on a time when obeying God felt risky or counterintuitive. What fears or hesitations did you face, and how did you overcome them?

What is one area of obedience you feel God calling you to focus on in the coming months? How can you prepare your heart and mind to respond faithfully?

Imagine a future where you live out complete obedience to God. What does that look like, and what changes would you need to start making today?

pray

Dearest Redemptive God, give me a faith like Noah. I confess that at times I struggle to trust in Your promises. I let fear get the best of me, and I don't always believe You have my best intentions in mind. But help me to remember that Your "commands leads to eternal life" (John 12:50). You are for my flourishing, and propel me into a flourishing life. You desire abundant life for me, and offer it in yourself. So today, I surrender at the altar of Your commands once again. I surrender my fears and selfishness and mistrust and doubt. I offer it up believing that by Your grace and mercy these things will be replaced with peace and sacrifice and trust that leads to obedience. Amen.

Obedience is key
to any covenant gifted by
God to humanity.

day 3

The Flood

Settle in, disciple. As sure as you are present in your space, so is Jesus. This moment, as fleeting as it may seem, is divinely orchestrated for you to hear from a loving God. Today, the invitation is one of trust and gentleness. In our study, we may feel the grief and judgment of God. The idea of punishment isn't a side of God we want to know, but we should know it because it is the judgment of sin by God that leads to our experience of the new humanity God makes possible. In the new humanity, we experience unity and communal life with God in person—we experience *shalom.*

When we turn to the end of Noah's story tomorrow, we will see God's mercy override His wrath and anger. But first, we discover wrath poured out on His creation.

Read and fill in the chart:

Read	Actions of God	Promises of God	Character Traits of God
Genesis 6:5–13, 17–18			
Genesis 7:1–4			
Genesis 8:1–5			

The story begins with a wayward world that grieves God deeply. God cannot tolerate the tortured relationship any longer. But God doesn't abandon His creation, He stays. The flood was all encompassing and destructive. The "high mountains" were even covered (Genesis 7:19). Everything Noah had known was now consumed by the waters. Nothing escaped. First comes death, then redemption.

How does the story of the flood demonstrate both God's judgment and His protection?

> Walter Brueggemann writes concerning the flood story, "But the gospel of this God is that he remembers. The only thing the waters of chaos and death do not cut through (though they cut through everything else) is the commitment of God to creation. His remembering is an act of gracious engagement with His covenant partner, an act of committed compassion. It asserts that God is not preoccupied with Himself but with His covenant partner, creation. It is the remembering of God, and only that, which gives hope and makes new life possible."[1]

The story of the flood is marked by both catastrophic destruction and the renewal of life. Reflect on why God chose to save Noah and his family instead of erasing all humanity and starting anew.

What does this decision tell you about God's commitment to His creation and His redemptive plan?

1 Walter Brueggemann, *Genesis, Interpretation* (Atlanta: Knox , 1982), 85.

What does the preservation of a remnant reveal about God's understanding of the intrinsic goodness of what He initially created?

How does the flood narrative expand your understanding of God's long-term covenant relationship with humanity?

Waiting is such a common theme in the lives of those who follow God throughout Scripture. What might God be teaching us through these periods of waiting without a clear end?

Tomorrow, we will see the God who remembers, loves, and redeems. But today is the in-between. Much like the disciples waited at the tomb where Jesus' dead body lay, so we also will wait to read about the redeeming work of God tomorrow. Hope is on the way, beloved. God remembers.

pray

Write a prayer to God thanking Him for His remembrance of you and His people.

day 4

The Reversal

God's mercy is new every day. Today, as you prepare to rest in God's presence, let's begin by thanking God for His unending mercy. Open your heart and mind and, in your own words, write a prayer below praying for the mercy of God to revive any dullness or dimness in your heart.

read

Genesis 8:20–9:17

study

Now that Noah reaches dry ground, his first act is that of worship. Worship is the right response to the salvific work of God. God spared Noah's life, and this spontaneous worship is a sign of Noah's overwhelming gratitude.

Up until now, we have seen the redemptive nature of God. God was the first to extend grace, and in response, Noah worshiped. The focus is on the action, goodness, and grace of God. David Peterson writes,

> "Acceptable worship does not start with human inventiveness, but with the action of God. The earliest books of the Bible emphasize God's initiative in revealing his character and will to his people, rescuing them from other lords in order to serve him exclusively, and establishing the pattern of response by which their relationship with him could be maintained."[2]

We learn in Scripture and experience for ourselves that God is the true initiator of worship and calls us into the lifestyle of worship. God is the one who takes the initiative to make Himself known to His people, and when we encounter the unending grace of God, how could we not worship? In this way, each of us experiences just what Noah did.

Consider the action of God in your own life. Make a list of how God has extended grace and goodness and kindness.

- ____________________
- ____________________
- ____________________

Write a prayer of worship in your own words.

2 Peterson, David G. *Engaging With God: A Biblical Theology of Worship.* InterVarsity Press, 2002, pg. 26.

We began the week by reflecting on the wickedness of humanity. As we discovered, it wasn't God who pulled the thread that led to an unraveling of sin and brokenness, but it was Adam and Eve and their offspring who pulled that thread—it was humanity, it was you and me, *it was us*. But the Noahic Covenant brings about a stunning reversal.

Read and fill in the chart:

Read	Commands to Adam	Commands to Noah
Genesis 1:26–31		
Genesis 9:1–7		

What similarities do you notice about the commands given to Adam and Noah?

In the commentary on the book of Genesis, Kenneth Mathews helps us see that Noah is depicted as the revived Adam.

> "As the sole survivor and successor to Adam; both 'walk' with God; both are recipients of the promissory blessing; both are caretakers of the lower creatures; both father three sons; both are workers of the soil; both sin through the fruit of a tree; and both father a wicked son who is under a curse. . . . The Lord 'put' Adam in Eden as the divine ideal for man, but

> because of the sin of the soil is man's new opponent . . . we can only view Noah through the template of Adam, both the promise and the garden sin."[3]

As Noah and Adam walked with God, you are also invited to walk with God.

What does walking with God look like in your life?

____

____

____

____

We are reminded, then, that in the beginning pages of Scripture, God is a God of fresh starts, new beginnings, and revival. So it is with you. No matter where you have been or what you've done or what you've been through, God's thread line of mercy doesn't skip over you, but it lands on you and weaves you into **His**tory.

Perhaps this is a moment of revival or new beginnings for you. It can begin now.

Make a worshipful and honest list of areas in your life where you are longing for revival:

- ______________________________________
- ______________________________________
- ______________________________________
- ______________________________________
- ______________________________________
- ______________________________________

3 Kenneth A. Mathews, *Genesis 1–11:26, New American Commentary* (Nashville: Broadman & Holman, 1996), 393.

pray

Dearest Redemptive God, I know You don't owe me anything. I know that I have lived a corrupt life, and my heart is more wicked than I often care to confess. But I know that new beginnings must begin somewhere. So I confess that my heart is hard. I confess that I haven't always loved You with my whole heart. I confess that I fail to love my neighbor as You call me to. I know that I am selfish and prideful, so God, I lay it all down at the altar of grace. If nothing else, I desire mercy and Your tender-loving presence. Just as You did a new thing in Noah's life, may it be so in me. Revive me. Heal me. Redeem me. Take me back to my first love. God, I am Yours. Amen.

"Acceptable worship does not start with human inventiveness, but with the action of God."[4]

4 Peterson, David G. *Engaging With God: A Biblical Theology of Worship.* InterVarsity Press, 2002, pg. 26.

day 5

guided contemplative prayer

read

Psalm 136:1–9

reflect

1. What aspects of God's character are highlighted in this psalm?
2. How does reflecting on God's enduring love and faithfulness impact your faith?

guided prayer exercise

preparation

- Light a candle and find a quiet space.
- Close your eyes and take a few deep breaths to center yourself.

meditation

- Focus on the candle flame as a symbol of God's light and presence.
- Slowly read Psalm 136:1–9 aloud, emphasizing the refrain "His love endures forever."

reflection

- Spend a few minutes reflecting on each verse, considering how you have experienced God's love and faithfulness in your life.

breath prayer

- Breathe in: "God of mercy."
- Breathe out: "Hold me in Your grace."

closing prayer

- Thank God for His enduring love and faithfulness. Ask Him to help you live in the light of His promises.

journaling

- On the next page, write a prayer of gratitude for God's faithfulness.
- Reflect on how His promises have shaped your life and faith.

journaling prayer

Session 2

The Covenant with Abraham

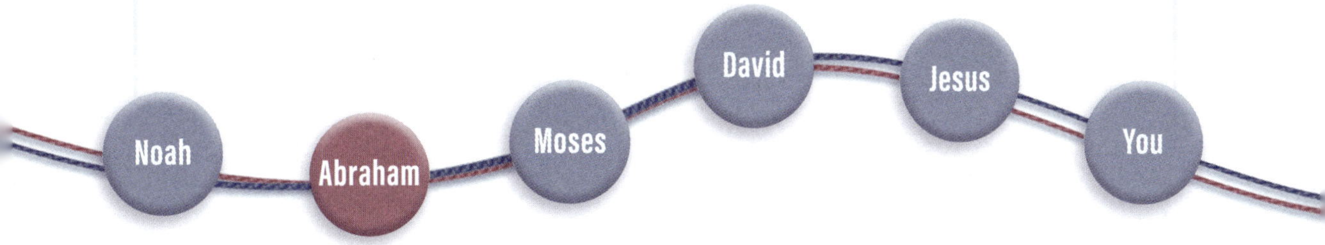

group session (90 minutes)

icebreaker and opening

What is the biggest leap of faith you've ever taken in your life?

Select a volunteer to read the following aloud to your group:

> Last week we dove into the depths of the Noahic Covenant and discovered the God who will never leave or forsake his people, no matter what. Noah, no doubt, took leaps of trust without knowing where God would lead. This week, we delve into another journey of blind faith. The thread of promise did not end with Noah, but it weaves into an expanded covenant beginning with a nomad by the name of Abram, who will later be called Abraham (Genesis 17:5). While he is called Abram early in the story, we will refer to him as Abraham throughout for the sake of ease in our discussion below.

Abraham's story is one of radical trust and obedience to God's promises. As a nomad with no clear idea of where God was leading him, Abraham stepped into the unknown based solely on God's promise. He took a leap of faith, trusting in the promise of God's blessing despite the impossibility of his circumstances.

As you prepare to dive into the Abrahamic Covenant, open your heart to where God may be asking you to trust Him, even when the outcome feels uncertain or impossible. Pray together in unison or select a volunteer to read for your group. Commit yourselves to hearing from the Lord as you go through this study and seek Him continually.

prayer

Dearest Covenant God, we give thanks for Your faithfulness to Your promises. As we journey into the story of Abraham, we ask that You open our hearts to the ways You are calling us into deeper trust in You. Let us have the courage to step out in faith, knowing that You are the God who fulfills every promise. Amen.

read before watching

Ask a volunteer to read Genesis 12:1–4 and 15:1–6 aloud before watching the video.

Abraham's story is one of radical trust and obedience to God's promises.

video

watch video session 2 (23 minutes)
The Covenant with Abraham

Leader, stream the video using access instructions on the inside front cover, or play the DVD (sold separately).

notes

Use this space to take notes from the teaching if you like.

group discussion

(40 minutes)

Leader, read the following prompts to the group for discussion.

Tara Beth unpacked the covenant God made with Abraham, emphasizing God's promise of blessing and the leap of faith Abraham took. We also explored Abraham's doubts in waiting for God's promises to be fulfilled.

1. **Reflect on a time when you took a leap of faith, trusting God even when the future seemed uncertain. Share your experience with the group.**

God's promise to Abraham was not only for him but for all the nations.

2. **How does this promise impact your understanding of God's heart for the world today?**

In Genesis 15, Abraham expresses doubt about God's promise because he and his wife Sarah (originally known as Sarai) are childless.

3. **Have you ever felt like God was taking too long to fulfill a promise? How can Abraham's story encourage us in moments of doubt?**

God's promise to Abraham continues the theme of restoring *shalom in creation*.

4. **How does Abraham's story connect with the grand narrative of redemption that we explored last week in the covenant with Noah?**

Turn to Hebrews 11:8–12 and have a volunteer read aloud to the group.

5. **How does the author of Hebrews describe Abraham's faith? What lessons can we draw from his unwavering trust in God's promises?**

6. **What responsibilities did Abraham have under this covenant, and how do these responsibilities shape our worldview as Christians today?**

God's promise to Abraham was not only for him but for all the nations.

7. **How does this promise expand your understanding of God's mission in the world today? What role do we as Christians play in continuing this blessing to the nations?**

Have a volunteer read Galatians 3:7–9 aloud to the group.

8. **How does Paul connect the Abrahamic covenant with the spreading of the gospel to all nations? How does this shift our perspective on the church's mission today?**

closing reflection

Leader, read these prompts to the group and provide some time for reflection and response.

- What is one key takeaway from today's discussion that you will carry with you this week?
- How can we pray for each other to grow in our understanding and application of God's promises and faithfulness?

close in prayer

Take turns reading paragraphs of this closing prayer.

Heavenly Father,

We come before You today as Your covenant people, grateful for the rich promises You have spoken over our lives, promises that stretch back to Abraham and find their fulfillment in Jesus. Lord, we stand in awe of Your faithfulness, Your unwavering presence in every twist and turn of our journey. You are a God who never abandons, never forsakes, never wastes a moment of our story, no matter how broken or uncertain it feels.

Today, we bring before You the moments of doubt, the seasons of waiting, the times when our faith feels frail and our hearts grow weary. Just as You met Abraham in his doubts and uncertainty, meet us here in ours. Strengthen us, God, for the journey ahead. Help us to trust, not in our own plans, but in Your divine purpose, even when the road is long, even when the way seems unclear.

Lord, we ask for Your Holy Spirit to empower us to live out the promises You've spoken into our lives. Make us a blessing to those around us. Let the world see in us the light of Christ, a people set apart to bring shalom, to be agents of Your Kingdom, to carry Your love to the nations.

God, we acknowledge that we cannot do this on our own. We need Your grace, Your strength, Your wisdom, and Your courage. Remind us daily of the covenant we are invited into—one of deep love, relentless grace, and never-ending hope. Help us to be bold, to step out in faith like Abraham, trusting that You are writing a story far greater than we can imagine.

As we go from this place, we ask that You would go before us. Open our eyes to see where You are at work in the world around us and open our hearts to join You there. May we live as covenant people in faith, in hope, and in love for Your glory and for the sake of Your Kingdom.

We pray all of this in the mighty and matchless name of Jesus, our King and Redeemer. Amen.

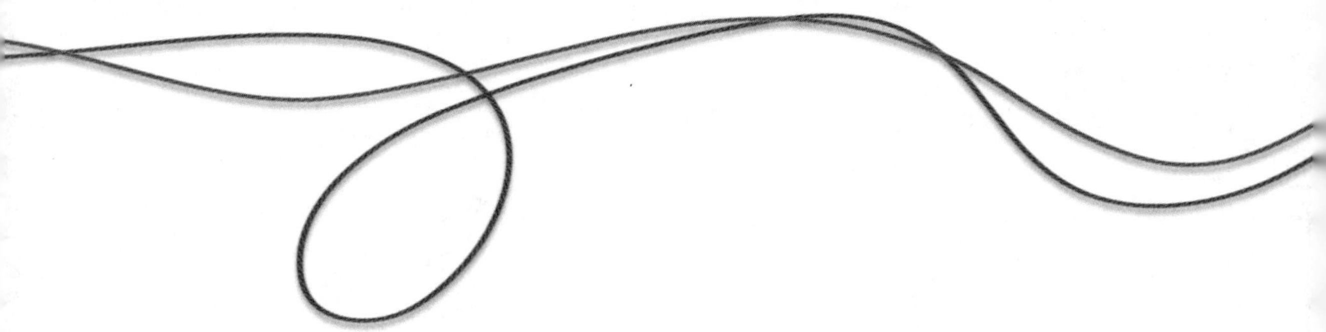

Session 2

personal Bible study

The Covenant with Abraham

day 1

God's Call to Abraham

Wherever you find yourself this week—in a coffee shop or a cubicle or a quiet nook in your home—settle in, beloved. God is a God that meets us in all places of life, and God is with you now. Begin by taking a few moments to pray for awareness of God's presence:

> *God, I thank You for Your presence. I thank You especially for Your kindness that You would meet me in this space. Help me to quiet my mind so that I might absorb any word You have for me. Please highlight words or phrases that could lead to clarity or transformation in my own heart and mind. Help me to quiet my mind and soul so that I might hear from You. Give me the grace to focus and a sound mind to understand Your word. Amen.*

read

Genesis 12:1–9

study

The call of Abraham is central not just to the book of Genesis, but to the entire redemptive story of God. Earlier in Genesis, God made a unilateral and unconditional promise to Noah and all living creatures that He would never again destroy the earth with a flood. We can trust in the divine promise that catastrophe will not come from God again. Although the stage of mercy and patience has unfolded, God has not yet addressed the deeper issue of human sinfulness. The Abrahamic Covenant is a grand leap toward God's plan of salvation and redemption.

This thread line is one of blessing, and today we experience its fruits in innumerable ways. It all begins with God's promise to one man and his descendants.

As the Bible progresses, we will see these promises repeated and developed in various places, but here in Genesis 12:1–3, they are introduced as a whole, setting the foundation for God's unfolding plan of salvation.

What were God's specific promises to Abraham in Genesis 12:2–3?

The promises are bunched together into three strands: land, seed, and blessing. These promises are repeated elsewhere, but only here do we see these three promises combined. At first glance, we do not recognize the weight of this promise given to Abram, a man with no land and no offspring.

These three promises—**land, seed,** and **blessing**—are closely linked. Abraham's descendants will inherit the land, where they will become a great nation, and through them God's blessing will reach the whole world.

Land: The promise of land becomes central during the exodus narrative as the people of Israel move toward the land of Canaan, receive it as their inheritance, eventually lose it due to their disobedience, and hope for its restoration.

Seed (Descendants): Abraham's descendants, the people of Israel, become the focus of the Old Testament, and through them the Messiah (Jesus) comes to bring salvation.

Blessing: While God blesses Abraham and his family, the ultimate blessing is that through Jesus, the entire world is invited into a relationship with God and receives redemption.

For this promise to come to fruition, however, Abraham's obedience was required.

What stands out to you about Abraham's response to God's call?

What was the cost of his obedience?

reflect

Write about a time when you felt God calling you to something unknown. How did you respond, and what did you learn about God's faithfulness in that season?

How do you typically respond to God when He asks you to take risks or make sacrifices? Do you hesitate or do you trust His plan?

pray

Lord, just as You called Abraham, I believe You are calling me today to walk in courageous faith. Even when things aren't clear, I want to ruthlessly trust and follow You. Help me to respond with faith, trusting in Your promises. Lead me to deeper trust and surrender, knowing that Your plans are for my good. Amen.

day2

God's Promise of Blessing

Beloved, God's promise to Abraham was not just for him, but it was a promise for all generations until the end of time. What we will discover in this study is that blessing is about restoring what was lost in the garden of Eden. In a world that is utterly fraught with difficulty, God chose a family where blessing can be embodied, even in a weary world. As you relax into God's Word, may kind blessings of God find you in your places of weariness today.

read

Genesis 15:1–6

study

In what way does the phrase "the word of the Lord came to Abram (that is, Abraham)" indicate the significance of divine revelation in the Old Testament? How does this phrase elevate the authority of what follows?

Below, record the promises of God in each verse:

Read	God's Promises
Genesis 15:1	
Genesis 15:2–4	
Genesis 15:5	

How does Abraham's question to God in Genesis 15:2 reflect his concern about the covenant promise from Genesis 12? Reread Genesis 12:1–9 if you need to refresh your memory.

What theological concern or question is Abraham wrestling with here, considering God's earlier promise of descendants?

The promise of a biological heir is a stunning and redemptive thread that leads to and reaches its climax in King Jesus, the light of the world. This isn't just a promise that extends to one, six, or even one hundred generations—it is a promise that extends through all eternity. God's allusion to the stars in Genesis 15:5 represents the vast reach of God's promise to restore humanity.

read

Galatians 3:7–9

How does the promise of blessing extend to us today as spiritual descendants of Abraham?

How does Genesis 15:6 mark a key turning point in understanding faith and righteousness?

Abraham being credited righteous by faith alone is a key theological principle for the people of God. It is a reminder that we are never saved by works but by the action of God and our response of faith. How does this reminder shape your understanding of salvation and your relationship with God? Take a few moments to reflect on how this theological truth influences your view of faith and your walk with God.

reflect

How does the example of Abraham's faith in Genesis 15:1–6 challenge or encourage you to trust God with the seemingly impossible areas of your life, and how might you respond to God's promises with deeper faith today?

pray

Dearest Lord, like Abraham, we often wrestle with doubt and wonder how Your promises will come to pass. But today, we choose to trust You, knowing that You are our shield and our very great reward. Help us to lean into Your faithfulness, to believe in Your goodness even when circumstances seem impossible. Strengthen our faith, that it may be credited to us as righteousness, not by our works but by our trust in You.

Guide us, Lord, to walk in step with Your promises. May our faith grow deeper, and may we respond to Your calling with boldness and surrender. We thank You for being the God who sees, the God who provides, and the God who fulfills every word. In all things, we look to You as our hope and our source of life. Amen.

day 3

The Struggle of Waiting

Waiting is hard. It brings us face to face with our own impatience, our desire for control, and our struggle to trust. But in the waiting, God does some of His most transformative work, dear one. In the waiting, He refines our faith, shapes our character, and reminds us that His promises are not dependent on our efforts but on His faithfulness.

God *is* faithful. Always. Forever.

As we enter into this study, we're invited to sit with the discomfort of waiting alongside Sarah and Abraham. But we're also invited to hear God's voice, reminding us that He is El Shaddai—God Almighty—the One who fulfills His promises in His time. I pray that as we walk through this text together, we might learn to surrender our impatience, trust His timing, and believe that He is still at work, even in the waiting. And when we are waiting, God is threading a redemptive story in our lives that we may not see—God is weaving all things together for our and His good.

read

Genesis 16:1–4; 17:1–8

Waiting can be agonizing. Whether it's waiting for a promise to be fulfilled, a prayer to be answered, or a dream to be realized, the experience of waiting often feels like an endless stretch of uncertainty. And when the waiting stretches on, it's easy for doubt to creep in. We wonder if God has forgotten us or if we somehow misunderstood His plan.

Sarah and Abraham were two people caught in the tension of waiting. God had promised them descendants, but years passed, and the promise seemed far from being fulfilled. They grew weary. Sarah's pain deepened as she wrestled with the reality of her barrenness, and in her desperation she took God's redemptive thread into her own hands.

What does Sarah's plan to give her servant, Hagar, to Abraham reveal about her understanding of God's promise?

read

Proverbs 3:5–6

Reflect on the contrast between Sarah's actions and the wisdom offered in these verses. Use the space below to write what you might say to Sarah about wisdom if given the chance.

study

Look back again at Genesis 17:1–8.

What does God reaffirm to Abraham in these verses?

In 17:1, God introduces Himself to Abraham as El Shaddai (God Almighty).

What significance does this name carry in the context of Abraham's doubt and the long wait for God's promise?

Look up Isaiah 40:28–31.

How does this passage echo the power and faithfulness of God Almighty?

In Genesis 17:5–8, God changes Abram's name to Abraham, signifying a new identity and a greater purpose.

How does this act of renaming Abram reflect God's continued faithfulness to His promise despite Abraham's previous mistakes?

Look up 2 Corinthians 5:17.

How does this idea of new identity through God's work connect to the larger story of redemption in your life?

When God speaks to Abraham in Genesis 17, He is not just repeating a promise. He is reweaving Abraham's identity into His greater story of redemption. "I am God Almighty," He says—El Shaddai, the One who sustains, provides, and holds all things together. He reminds Abraham that the covenant is not based on human effort but on *divine faithfulness*.

The name change from Abram to Abraham signals something powerful: God is still at work, still threading together His story, even when Abraham might have felt like things had come unraveled. Just as Abraham's identity was transformed by God's covenant, we too are given new names and new identities in Christ. Our stories are also woven into His great redemptive tapestry.

reflect

Can you identify moments in your life when you've tried to take control of the situation rather than trusting God's timing? How did that work out for you? What might God be inviting you to trust Him with today?

God is threading together a story that leads to His redemptive purposes. In the moments when we cannot see the full picture, may we trust that the Master Weaver is still at work. Let's dive in, knowing that God's promise is still unfolding.

pray

Write out your own prayer. Ask God, the Master Weaver, to develop a posture of trust in God's larger plan.

day 4

God's Covenant Sealed

As you enter into this study, ask yourself: Where is God asking me to trust Him more deeply? What does it mean for me to live as one marked by faith, not just outwardly but inwardly, in every part of my life? Together, let's seek to understand how God's covenant, first given to Abraham, is still at work in us today, as He continues weaving His promises through the threads of our lives.

Let's approach this study with open hearts, ready to see how God is inviting us into a deeper, faith-filled journey in His story of redemption.

read

Genesis 17:1–14

study

As we enter this study, we find ourselves standing in a place where God is stitching together a story far greater than we can imagine. It's a story of promise and covenant, one that threads through generations, from Abraham to us today. The physical sign of circumcision may seem strange to us at first, but behind it is a profound truth about what it means to be set apart by God.

In Genesis 17 God gives Abraham a sign—a mark of His covenant that will physically distinguish Abraham's descendants as God's people. But what we must see is that circumcision was the external reflection of the internal reality and relationship of faithfulness God desired for His people.

Circumcision points to something deeper: God is always about transforming hearts, shaping His people, and drawing us into His redemptive plan. As we dig in, let's also look forward to the fulfillment of this covenant in Christ. The apostle Paul helps us see that the real marker of belonging to God is *faith*. It's faith that makes us part of God's family. The outward signs—whether circumcision in Abraham's time or baptism in ours—are simply expressions of an inner transformation. God is threading together a story of redemption, one in which faith, not rituals, is what truly sets us apart as His people.

In Genesis 17:1–14, God introduces circumcision as the physical sign of His covenant with Abraham and his descendants.

Why do you think God chose a physical sign for this covenant?

Look up Deuteronomy 30:6.

How does circumcision point to a deeper spiritual reality?

Look up Galatians 3:28–29.

In what ways does this covenantal sign expand the threadline and move into the New Testament to include all believers in Christ?

Read Romans 4:13–25.

How does Paul explain the importance of Abraham's faith in God's promises, even before the covenant was sealed with circumcision?

Use the chart below to draw the parallels between the sign of circumcision in Genesis 17 and the role of faith described in Romans 4.

Genesis 17:1–14	Romans 4:13–25
What Does Circumcision Signify?	What Does Faith Look Like in a Believer's Life?

How does faith become the marker by which we enter God's covenant promises?

reflect

Consider the ways you "mark" your own relationship with God. What outward signs or practices help you live into your covenant relationship with Him?

pray

Gracious and faithful God,

My heart is filled with gratitude for the way You have been weaving Your story of redemption through history and into my life. I thank You for the covenant You made with Abraham, for the promise that extends to me through faith in Christ, and for the reminder that I am marked by Your grace through trust in You, not by my own efforts.

Lord, help me to live as someone set apart by faith—someone who trusts in Your promises, even when I cannot see the full picture. Strengthen my faith when doubt creeps in, and remind me that You are always at work, threading together something far greater than I can imagine.

As I go from this time of study, may I carry with me the knowledge that I am part of Your family, marked by the faith You have given me. Let me live as one who reflects Your covenant love, sharing the hope of Your promises with a world that longs to know You. Amen.

day 5

guided contemplative prayer

read

Read:

Psalm 105:1–11

reflect:

1. What stands out to you about God's faithfulness in this psalm?
2. How do you see yourself woven into God's holy promise given to the "descendants of Abraham"?

guided prayer exercise

preparation

- Light a candle to remind yourself of God's presence.
- Take a few deep breaths to quiet your heart.

meditation

- Focus on the theme of faith and promise as you read Psalm 105 aloud.

reflection

- Reflect on a time when God's faithfulness was evident in your life.

breath prayer

- Breathe in: "God of promises."
- Breathe out: "I trust in You."

closing prayer

- Thank God for the promise of blessing through Abraham.

journaling

- On the next page, write a prayer of gratitude for God's promises and reflect on how they have shaped your faith.

journaling prayer

Session 3

The Covenant with Moses

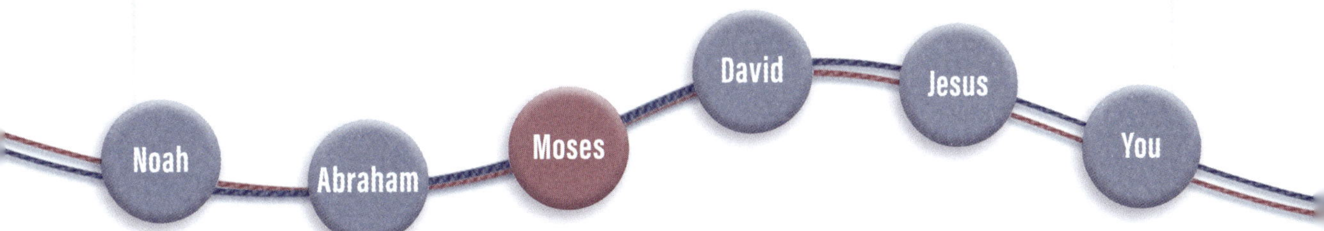

group session (90 minutes)

icebreaker and opening

What's one rule or law that isn't fun to follow, but you do it because it brings order or fairness?

Select a volunteer to read the following aloud to your group:

> Last week, we explored God's covenant with Abraham—a promise that required radical trust and faith in the unknown. Today, we move from a covenant God made with one man to a covenant He made with an entire nation. The thread of God's promise weaves through the story of the Israelites as they are led out of slavery in Egypt and brought to the foot of Mount Sinai under the leadership of Moses, where they receive what comes to be known as the Mosaic Covenant. This covenant outlines the law that would shape the Israelite's identity and relationship with God as His chosen people.

The Mosaic Covenant is about more than laws and regulations; it is about *God's desire for a holy people, set apart to reflect His heart to the world*. As we enter into this study, let us open our hearts to the ways God is calling us to live faithfully within His covenant, recognizing that even today He is threading together His story of redemption through our lives.

Let's prepare to listen to His voice as we reflect on the meaning of this covenant and what it means for us as followers of Christ.

prayer

Select a volunteer or pray together in unison:

Covenant God, we come before You with open hearts as we dive into the story of the Mosaic Covenant. Just as You gave Israel Your laws to live by, we ask that You show us how to walk faithfully in Your ways. May Your Spirit guide us as we seek to understand Your will and live as a people set apart for Your purposes. Amen.

read before watching

Ask a volunteer to read Exodus 19:3–6 and 20:1–17 before watching the video.

The Mosaic Covenant is about more than laws and regulations; it is about God's desire for a holy people, set apart to reflect His heart to the world.

video

watch video session 3 (19:30 minutes)
The Covenant with Moses

Leader, stream the video using access instructions on the inside front cover, or play the DVD (sold separately).

notes

Use this space to take notes from the teaching if you like.

group discussion
(40 minutes)

Leader, read the following prompts to the group for discussion.

Tara Beth unpacked the Mosaic Covenant, emphasizing God's law given to Moses and how it defined Israel's relationship with God. We also explored the deeper meaning of the law in shaping the identity of God's people.

God's rescue comes first.

1. **Reflect on how God first rescued the Israelites before giving them the law. How does the order of God's actions help us understand the role of obedience in our relationship with God today?**

God's covenant at Sinai was meant to set Israel apart as a "kingdom of priests" and a "holy nation" (Exodus 19:6).

2. **What does it mean for you today to live as part of a holy people, set apart for God's purposes?**

The Ten Commandments outline the core of the Mosaic Covenant.

3. **How do these commandments reflect God's desire for justice, mercy, and righteousness in the world? In what ways do you see these values shaping our society today—or areas where they are lacking?**

The Israelites faced challenges in living out the law faithfully.

4. **Look at your own life. Are there commandments or areas of obedience that feel especially difficult to follow? How does God's grace help us when we fall short of His standards?**

The Mosaic Covenant is a continuation of God's desire to restore shalom in creation.

5. How does the giving of the law point forward to Jesus, the One who would fulfill the law?

6. Look at Romans 8:1–4 and discuss how Christ transforms our understanding of the law today.

God's law was both a gift and a responsibility.

7. With the Mosaic Covenant in mind, how can we reflect the heart of God's law in our daily lives, not as legalistic rules but as a reflection of God's character?

God called the Israelites to be a kingdom of priests, mediating His blessing to the world.

8. How are we, as Christians, called to mediate God's blessing, love, and *shalom* today?

closing reflection

Leader, read these prompts to the group and provide some time for reflection and response.

- What is one key takeaway from today's discussion that you will carry with you this week?
- How can we pray for each other to grow in our understanding and application of God's covenant and His law?

close in prayer

Read aloud together or select a volunteer to pray over your group:

Dearest Faithful God, we thank You for your covenant with Moses and the way you have called your people to live as a light to the nations. We ask for your grace to walk faithfully in the ways you've shown us, not out of obligation but out of love for you and for others. Guide us as we reflect your justice, mercy, and holiness in our world. Amen.

The Mosaic Covenant is a continuation of God's desire to restore shalom in creation.

Session 3

personal Bible study

The Covenant with Moses

day 1

God's Promise to Moses

As we enter this personal study on the Mosaic Covenant, pause for a moment and think about what it means to be set apart. In our everyday lives, we may not often think about being "set apart" or "holy," but this is exactly what God was calling the Israelites to be in the wilderness at Mount Sinai.

Imagine the scene: an entire nation freshly delivered from slavery, standing at the foot of a mountain, trembling as God speaks. God then calls them to be a people who reflect His heart, His justice, and His holiness to the world.

But this wasn't just about rules; it was about *relationship*. It was about God's deep desire to thread His people into His redemptive plan for all creation.

In the same way, God calls us today to live in this covenant relationship. As we explore Exodus 19:1–6, I invite you to reflect on the profound truth that God has set you apart to live in His story. He has called you to reflect His heart, His justice, and His love in the world.

read

Exodus 19:1–6

Exodus 19:1–6 is one of the most powerful and pivotal moments in the biblical narrative. It is where God brings the Israelites to Mount Sinai and establishes a covenant that will shape their identity as His people. In these verses, God reminds Israel of how He delivered them from Egypt, describing His action with the tender image of carrying them on "eagles' wings." This metaphor speaks of God's strength, care, and sovereignty in rescuing His people from oppression. The image of an eagle carrying its young emphasizes God's protective guidance, showing that it was His divine power, not human effort, that secured their freedom.

Theologically, this passage marks a significant development in the relationship between God and His people. In calling them His "treasured possession," a "kingdom of priests," and a "holy nation," God isn't simply giving them new titles—He's offering them a new identity and purpose. The covenant calls Israel to a life that reflects God's holiness and His desire to restore *shalom* (peace and wholeness) to all of creation. As a kingdom of priests, the Israelites are to mediate God's presence to the world, showing His character of justice, mercy, and love. This calling is not limited to their own benefit but is meant to extend beyond them, fulfilling God's promise to Abraham that all nations would be blessed through his descendants.

study

In Exodus 19:4, God reminds the Israelites of how He carried them out of Egypt "on eagles' wings" and brought them to Himself. This beautiful imagery speaks of God's protection and tender care.

Why do you think God reminded the Israelites of His deliverance before calling them into covenant?

Look up Deuteronomy 7:6–8.

How are God's deliverance and covenant linked?

In Exodus 19:5–6, God gives Israel a powerful identity—His *treasured possession*, *a kingdom of priests*, and a *holy nation*. These titles highlight both privilege and responsibility. Israel is called to reflect God's character and to mediate His presence in the world.

What does it mean to be a "kingdom of priests" and a "holy nation"?

Look up 1 Peter 2:9–10 and reflect on how this calling applies to believers today.

How does this connect with your understanding of the church's mission in your neighborhood and in the world?

The covenant in Exodus 19:5 comes with a call to *obey fully*. God's covenant is not just a promise but also a relationship that requires faithfulness on the part of His people.

How does obedience factor into our relationship with God today?

Look up John 15:9–11.

Think through how Jesus speaks about obedience and its connection to love and joy and reflect on what Jesus' words mean for living out God's covenant.

Who do you sense Jesus is calling you to love, and how will you fully obey him?

reflect

Just as God reminded the Israelites of His deliverance from Egypt, how has God carried you "on eagles' wings" in your life?

Identify a time when you've experienced God's deliverance and reflect on what it was like to be carried on God's wings.

pray

Close in prayer in your own words. Write out a prayer thanking God for deliverance in your own life.

day 2

The Gift of the Law

When we think about laws, we might first think of restrictions, boundaries, or things that hold us back. But when God gave the Israelites the Ten Commandments, He wasn't burdening them with rules. He was giving them a gift—a way of life that would bring them into deeper relationship with Him and with one another.

At Sinai, God gave a vision for what it meant to live as His holy people. The Ten Commandments weren't meant to be a list of dos and don'ts but rather an invitation to a flourishing life under God's care and direction. Each commandment is like a thread in the fabric of God's greater story of redemption. These laws not only reveal God's character but also show us how we can live in harmony with Him and with others.

As we reflect on the Ten Commandments today, let's approach them as a gift, not a burden. God is still inviting us into this way of life, calling us to live set apart in love, justice, and truth.

read

Exodus 20:1–17

study

The Ten Commandments are often seen as the core of the Mosaic law, providing the foundation for how God's people are to live in covenant with Him.

Before giving the commandments, God reminds the Israelites of who He is:

> "I am the Lord your God, who brought you out of Egypt" (Exodus 20:2).

This is a foundational truth—the Ten Commandments flow *out of Israel's* relationship with the God who has already saved them.

Why do you think God reminds Israel of His deliverance before giving the Ten Commandments?

How does this reminder frame the purpose of the law?

Look up Exodus 19:4–6.

Make a short list of how God's saving actions are connected to His call to obedience:

The first four commandments focus on Israel's relationship with God—honoring Him alone, denying all worship of idols, keeping His name and character holy, and resting in His presence on the Sabbath. These commandments call Israel to exclusive devotion to God.

What do the first four commandments reveal about God's character and His desire for our relationship with Him?

Look up Matthew 22:34–38.

Fill in the blank.

Jesus' teaching about loving God connects with the first four commandments in this way: ______________________________.

The remaining six commandments focus on how we are to live in relationship with others—honoring parents, avoiding murder, abstaining from adultery, refraining from theft, desisting from committing false witness, and not coveting. These commandments guide the community toward justice and peace.

How do these commandments shape our understanding of loving our neighbor?

Now look up Matthew 22:39–40.

Fill in the blank.

Jesus' teaching about loving neighbors connects with the remaining six commandments in this way: ______________________________.

reflect

Which commandment do you feel most challenged by today and why?

How might God be inviting you to live more fully in love toward Him or toward others?

pray

Spend a few moments in prayer, responding to what you've studied and reflected on. Here's a guide for your prayer:

- Thank God for the gift of His law, and for the ways it leads us into deeper relationship with Him and with others.
- Ask for the strength to live in love and holiness, reflecting God's character through your actions and attitudes.
- Pray for the wisdom to follow God's commandments, not out of duty but out of a desire to love and honor Him with your life.

day 3

A Kingdom of Priests

When God called the Israelites to Himself at Mount Sinai, He did more than give them a set of laws—He gave them a new identity. In Exodus 19:6, God calls Israel to be a "kingdom of priests and a holy nation." This wasn't just about following rules; it was about being set apart to represent God to the world. In ancient Israelite religion priests were mediators—those individuals who stood between God and the people, showing what God was like.

Fast forward to the New Testament, and Peter picks up this same language in 1 Peter 2:9–10. The church is now called a "royal priesthood" and a "holy nation." Just as Israel was called to reflect God's holiness and love to the world, so are we. The thread of the Mosaic Covenant runs right through to the church today. Our role as followers of Jesus is to live as priests who have been set apart to reveal the heart of God to a broken world. This calling is both a privilege and a responsibility.

As we explore what it means to be a "kingdom of priests," I invite you to pray about how God might be calling you to step into this role more fully in your life today.

read

1 Peter 2:9–10

study

The idea of a "kingdom of priests" is woven through both the Old and New Testaments. In the Mosaic Covenant, God called Israel to be His representatives in the world, a people who would reflect His holiness. Now, Peter applies that same identity to the church.

Both Exodus 19:5 and 1 Peter 2:9 use the language of being God's "special possession." This identity is rooted in God's covenant with His people, marking them as those set apart for His purposes. What does it mean to you personally that you are part of God's "chosen people" and "special possession"?

How does this shape your understanding of your relationship with God?

Look up Exodus 19:5.

How does this covenantal language apply to you today?

As part of God's kingdom of priests, Israel was called to represent God's character to the world. Priests were responsible for offering sacrifices, teaching the law, and leading the people in worship. In the New Covenant, this priestly role shifts to the church, but it still involves mediating God's presence and reflecting His heart to others.

Look up Hebrews 13:15–16.

In what ways do we offer spiritual sacrifices as part of our priestly role?

In 1 Peter 2:9–10, Peter emphasizes that this priestly calling is not just about living a set-apart life but also about declaring the praises of the One who has saved us. Our priesthood is about proclaiming God's goodness and His work of redemption.

What does it mean to "declare the praises" of God as part of your priestly identity?

How can you live this out practically in your daily life?

Look up Psalm 96:1–3.

Note a few ways you can declare God's goodness to those around you.

reflect

God has called you to be part of His "royal priesthood" and "holy nation." How does this identity challenge or encourage you in your walk with Christ? How can you live more fully into this calling in your workplace, home, or community?

pray

Gracious and Loving God,

Thank You for choosing me to be part of Your royal priesthood, for bringing me out of darkness and into Your marvelous light. I don't always feel worthy of this calling, but I know that it is by Your grace and mercy that I stand here as part of Your holy people.

Help me, Lord, to live fully into this identity. Show me how I can represent Your love, Your justice, and Your truth in my everyday life. Give me the courage to declare Your praises, not just with my words but with the way I live, so that others might see You through me.

I ask for strength to walk in this role as part of Your kingdom of priests. When I feel weak, remind me that You are with me, guiding and shaping me to be more like You. Let my life be a reflection of Your grace, a testimony of Your goodness in all that I do.

In Jesus' name I pray, amen.

When God called the Israelites to Himself at Mount Sinai, He did more than give them a set of laws—He gave them a new identity.

day 4

God's Covenant Confirmed

The confirmation of the covenant between God and Israel is a powerful moment in the story of redemption. After hearing the laws and commands of God at Mount Sinai, the people of Israel were faced with a choice: Would they enter into this covenant with God, agreeing to live as His holy and chosen people? This moment of decision, when the Israelites declare "we will do everything the Lord has said" (Exodus 24:3, 7) marks a profound step in their relationship with God. They're not just receiving God's laws—they are committing to live them out, affirming their identity as His covenant people.

As we reflect on this passage, I want to invite you to consider what it means to affirm your relationship with God. His covenant, confirmed through sacrifice and commitment, calls us into deeper relationship and obedience. Just as Israel stood at the foot of the mountain, we too are invited into a covenant relationship that shapes our lives and our identity. God's covenant isn't just a set of rules—it's an invitation to belong to Him and live as His treasured people.

read

Exodus 24:1–8

As you read through Exodus 24:1–8, you can sense the weight of this moment. God's covenant is not just an agreement made in passing—it's a profound commitment between the Creator and His people. The Israelites are standing at a crossroads, choosing to step into a binding relationship that will shape their identity and their lives. But this covenant comes with expectations and responsibility, and it will require sacrifice. Let's now dive deeper into what this covenant meant for Israel and what it reveals about our own commitment to God today.

Twice in this passage the people of Israel declare, "We will do everything the Lord has said." This is their formal acceptance of God's covenant, a commitment to live by the laws He has given them.

Why do you think the Israelites were in overwhelming and unanimous agreement to the covenant?

What does their wholehearted response teach us about the importance of responding to God's commands with obedience?

study

Look up Deuteronomy 30:19–20.

What stands out to you most about the choice Israel is given to choose life by following God's covenant?

The blood of the covenant plays a crucial role in sealing the agreement between God and His people. The blood, sprinkled on both the altar and the people, symbolized the seriousness of this covenant and the unity between God and Israel.

What is the significance of blood in this covenant ceremony? (If needed, return to your notes from the group session.)

Look up Hebrews 9:19–22.

Take note of the ways in which the blood of the covenant foreshadows the ultimate sacrifice of Christ.

Before confirming the covenant, Moses reads the "Book of the Covenant" to the people, reminding them of the laws and commands God has given. This is a moment of deep accountability—Israel knows what they are committing to.

How does hearing and understanding God's Word help us in our covenant relationship with Him today?

Look up James 1:22–25 and finish this sentence: It's important to not only hear God's Word but also to ____________________ .

In the space below, reflect on how you will obey that teaching in your own life.

reflect

Israel affirmed their commitment to God's covenant by saying, "we will obey."

What does obedience to God's covenant look like in your life? Are there areas where God is calling you to renew your commitment to Him?

prayer

Faithful and covenant-keeping God,

I thank You for the invitation to be in relationship with You, for the way You pursue us with Your love and grace. Just as You called Israel to commit themselves to You, You call me to a life of obedience and trust in Your promises. Help me to honor that call with a heart that is faithful, a heart that seeks to live out Your commands in all that I do.

I ask for the strength to follow You when it's difficult, and for the wisdom to understand Your Word more deeply. Thank You for the blood of the covenant, fulfilled in Christ, that secures this relationship with You. Guide me, Lord, in my daily walk, that I may reflect Your holiness and love in all areas of my life.

In Jesus' name I pray, amen.

day 5

guided contemplative prayer

read

Psalm 119:33–40

reflect

1. What does this psalm reveal about the psalmist's attitude toward God's law?
2. How can this attitude shape your approach to following God's commands?

guided prayer exercise

preparation

- Light a candle to remind yourself of God's presence.
- Take a few deep breaths to quiet your heart.

meditation

- Slowly read Psalm 119:33–40 aloud, reflecting on each verse.

reflection

- Spend a few moments considering how you can delight in God's law and live it out in your daily life.

breath prayer

- Breathe in: "Teach me your ways, Lord."
- Breathe out: "I delight in your law."

closing prayer

- Thank God for the gift of His law and ask for the strength to live according to His ways.

journaling

- On the next page, write a prayer of gratitude for God's commands and how they guide your life.

journaling prayer

Session 4

The Covenant with David

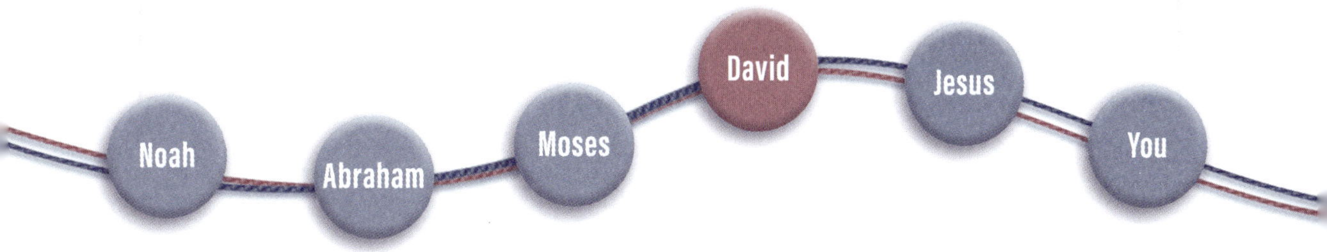

group session (90 minutes)

icebreaker and opening

What's one promise someone has made to you that had a significant impact on your life?

opening reflection

Select a volunteer to read the following aloud to your group:

Last week, we explored the covenant God confirmed with His people through Moses, a covenant rooted in law and relationship. Today, we're moving forward in the story of God's covenantal faithfulness, but this time through a promise made to a king—David. God's covenant with David points us toward something greater: an eternal kingdom that would be established through his descendants. This covenant doesn't just affect Israel, but it threads through the history of salvation and leads us to Jesus, the ultimate fulfillment of God's promise.

As we reflect on the Davidic Covenant, let's open our hearts to the reality of God's faithfulness. His promises aren't just for the past—they are alive and active in our lives today. What does it look like for us to trust in God's promises, even when we can't fully see the outcome?

prayer

Select a volunteer or pray together in unison:

Covenant-keeping God, we come before You with grateful hearts, trusting in the promises You have spoken over our lives. As we explore the covenant made with David today, may we gain a deeper understanding of Your faithful love. Open our hearts to the ways You are still establishing Your kingdom, both in us and through us. In Jesus' name, amen.

read before watching

Ask a volunteer to read 2 Samuel 7:8–16 aloud before watching the video.

His promises aren't just for the past—they are alive and active in our lives today.

video

watch video session 4 (23:30 minutes)
The Covenant with David

Leader, stream the video using access instructions on the inside front cover, or play the DVD (sold separately).

notes

Use this space to take notes from the teaching if you like.

group discussion

(40 minutes)

Leader, read the following prompts to the group for discussion.

Tara Beth unpacked the Davidic Covenant, focusing on God's promise to establish David's lineage and bring forth an eternal kingdom. She also explored how this covenant connects to God's greater plan of redemption through Jesus. Think of a time when you had to trust in a long-term promise. Share with the group what that experience was like.

1. **How does trusting in something yet to be fulfilled challenge your faith and patience?**

God promises David that his throne will be established forever.

2. **How does this promise impact your understanding of God's plans for Israel and for the world?**

3. **Look up Luke 1:29–33 and have someone read it out loud. How does Jesus fulfill this eternal promise?**

4. **Read David's response to God's promises in 2 Samuel 7:18–19 out loud. What can we learn from David's response about how we should react to God's promises in our own lives?**

5. **How does knowing that God is faithful to His promises shape our attitudes toward worship and obedience?**

God's covenant with David is part of the larger story of redemption that began with Abraham and flows through to the New Testament.

6. **How does the Davidic Covenant help us see the unfolding plan of God's kingdom?**

7. **Read Acts 13:21–23 out loud. How do the apostles understand this covenant and its fulfillment in Christ?**

8. **The Davidic Covenant shows us that God's promises are often fulfilled in ways we don't expect. How has God fulfilled promises in your life in ways that surprised you or looked different than what you had anticipated?**

closing reflection

Leader, read these prompts to the group and provide some time for reflection and response.

- What is one key takeaway from today's discussion that you will carry with you this week?
- How can we pray for each other to grow in our trust of God's promises, even when they take time to unfold?

close in prayer

Read aloud together or select a volunteer to pray over your group:

Dearest Faithful God, we thank You for the promises You made to David and the way You have been faithful to every word. Help us to trust in Your promises, knowing that You are always at work, even when we don't fully understand Your plans. Give us hearts that respond with humility and worship, just as David did. Strengthen us to live in faith, as we await the full establishment of Your kingdom in Jesus. Amen.

Session 4

personal Bible study

The Covenant with David

day 1

God's Promise to David

The covenant God made with David marks a pivotal moment in the story of God's redemptive plan. Up until this point, Israel had been led by judges, prophets, and a failed king named Saul. But here, God goes beyond merely establishing a king—God chooses the king Himself and promises to establish an eternal kingdom through him. This promise wasn't just about David's reign; it points to something much bigger. The kingdom God was establishing through David is the very kingdom Christians believe is come in Jesus, the eternal King.

According to 2 Samuel 7 David desired to build a house for God—a temple where His presence could dwell. Yet God turned this plan around and promised instead to build David a house—a royal dynasty. This covenant reflects God's desire to dwell with His people not through a physical building but through a lasting kingdom. God desires for His very presence to return to full communion with His people.

As you read and reflect on 2 Samuel 7:1–17, consider how God's promises are often larger and more far-reaching than we can imagine. God's covenant with David is not just about the past; it is a thread that weaves through history, pointing us toward Jesus and the fulfillment of God's eternal kingdom.

read

2 Samuel 7:1–17

As we step back from the reading, we can sense the weight of this moment for David. He desires to honor God, but God's plans are far greater than David could have imagined. Instead of a temple, God promises an enduring kingdom to David—a promise that stretches far beyond David's life and points to an eternal King. This passage invites us to reflect on the nature of God's promises, His sovereignty, and His unfolding plan of redemption. Let's now take a deeper look at how this covenant reveals God's faithfulness and how it connects to our lives today.

study

In this passage, God makes a covenant with David that reaches beyond his lifetime and points to an eternal kingdom. David feels settled and desires to honor God by building Him a permanent dwelling. Yet, God flips this plan, revealing that His presence cannot be contained by human efforts. God promises to establish a dynasty for David instead. Why do you think God shifted David's plan from building a temple to His plan in establishing a kingdom for David?

As a threadline in God's story, how does the Davidic Covenant reveal God's sovereignty and His greater plan?

Look up Isaiah 55:8–9.

How are God's ways higher than our ways?

God's covenant with David includes the promise of a lasting kingdom through his descendants. This promise points not only to Solomon, David's son, but ultimately to the Messiah, who would reign on David's throne forever.

How does the promise of an eternal kingdom connect to God's plan of salvation through the Messiah?

God assures David that His love will never be removed from his descendants, even when they sin and require discipline. This promise speaks of God's enduring faithfulness to His covenant, even when humans fall short (2 Samuel 7:15–16).

How does God's promise of discipline and steadfast love reflect His character?

Look up Hebrews 12:5–6.

In the space below, record your thoughts on how God's discipline is an expression of His love and commitment to His people.

reflect

Think of a time when you experienced God's faithfulness in your life. How does this memory help you trust in God's promises today?

pray

Dearest God of Promises, thank You for Your faithfulness. Help me trust in Your covenant, even when life feels uncertain. Remind me that Your promises endure, and I am part of Your eternal kingdom. Amen.

day2

The Eternal Kingdom

The covenant God made with David wasn't just a promise for his descendants—it was a promise for all of humanity. The promise of an eternal kingdom, fulfilled through a descendant of David, echoes throughout the biblical prophets and, as we'll see later, culminates in the arrival of Jesus. The books of Isaiah and Jeremiah both express this hope for what is yet to come. Both prophets point to a coming King, one who would rule with justice and righteousness forever.

As you read Isaiah 9:1–7 and Jeremiah 23:5–6, reflect on how these passages continue the thread of God's promise to David. The eternal kingdom is not just about political power or an earthly throne—it's about God's kingdom breaking into the world through His Son. This kingdom is one of peace, justice, and righteousness. It's a kingdom that you and I are invited into, living under the reign of the King of Kings.

read

Isaiah 9:1–7
Jeremiah 23:5–6

As we reflect on the words of Isaiah and Jeremiah, we see the unfolding of God's promise—a vision of a kingdom where justice and righteousness reign forever. These prophets pointed to a future hope, a King who would sit on David's throne and bring peace to the world. But this isn't just a promise for the distant future; it's a promise of a kingdom experience that is already available to us through Jesus. Now, let's dive deeper into these passages and explore how God's eternal kingdom is fulfilled in Christ and how it continues to shape our lives today.

study

In these Old Testament passages, the promise of an eternal kingdom is delivered through prophetic vision. Both Isaiah and Jeremiah speak of a coming King from the line of David who will bring righteousness, justice, and peace. This King is none other than Jesus, who we know as the fulfillment of God's covenant with David.

Both Isaiah and Jeremiah speak of a King who will rule with righteousness and justice, a King who will save His people and bring peace. How people will know of the fulfillment of the Davidic Covenant is through a final kingdom that will last forever, led by the Most High, righteous ruler.

How do these prophecies point to Jesus as the fulfillment of the Davidic Covenant?

Look up Luke 1:29–33.

Reflect on how the angel's message to Mary connects to these prophecies. In Isaiah 9:7, we see that "the zeal of the Lord Almighty will accomplish this." God is deeply committed to bringing about His kingdom, and His passion drives the fulfillment of His promises.

What does it mean that God's "zeal" will accomplish the establishment of His eternal kingdom?

How does the angel's message to Mary reveal God's unwavering commitment to His covenant promises?

Look up Philippians 1:6.

Consider how God's faithfulness to complete His work applies to your own life.

When you think of God's kingdom of justice, righteousness, and peace, how is that work being carried out through you?

In what specific ways can we live as citizens of this kingdom today?

Look up Matthew 6:33.

Make a list of some ways you are currently seeking God's kingdom and righteousness:

reflect

The kingdom of God is an eternal one, characterized by justice, righteousness, and peace. How do you experience God's kingdom in your life today? What does it look like to live under the reign of Jesus, the Righteous King?

pray

Spend a few moments in prayer, responding to what you've studied and reflected on. Here's a guide for your prayer:

- Thank God for the gift of His eternal kingdom and for sending Jesus to fulfill the promise of a righteous King.
- Ask for the wisdom and strength to live as a citizen of God's kingdom, reflecting His justice, righteousness, and peace in your life.
- Pray for a deeper understanding of what it means to seek first God's kingdom in your daily decisions and actions.

Both Isaiah and Jeremiah speak of a King who will rule with righteousness and justice, a King who will save His people and bring peace.

day 3

Jesus, the Fulfillment of the Covenant

Throughout the Old Testament, we see promises made. These are covenants established between God and His people. These promises, particularly the one made to David, pointed forward to something much greater: the coming of a King whose reign would last forever. In Jesus, we see the fulfillment of these ancient promises. He is the long-awaited King, the one who would establish God's eternal kingdom.

In Luke 1:29–33, the angel Gabriel announces to Mary that her child will inherit the throne of David, and His kingdom will never end. In Mark 1:14–15, Jesus begins His ministry by proclaiming that the kingdom of God is near. The promise of an eternal kingdom that began with David is fulfilled in Jesus. His arrival is the long-anticipated answer to the covenant God made with David—a kingdom that would be everlasting, one of justice, peace, and righteousness.

As we read these passages today, reflect on how Jesus fulfills the covenant promises of the Old Testament and brings God's eternal kingdom to earth. This isn't just a past event; it's a reality we live in today as citizens of His kingdom.

read

Luke 1:29–33
Mark 1:14–15

As we reflect on these passages, let's stand in awe of the faithfulness of God, who has fulfilled His covenant with David through Jesus. His kingdom has come near, and we are invited to live in the fullness of that reality today. May we walk as citizens of His eternal kingdom, trusting in the King who reigns forever.

Gabriel's message to Mary reveals that Jesus is the one who will inherit David's throne and rule over an eternal kingdom. This confirms that Jesus is the fulfillment of God's covenant with David.

How does the announcement of Jesus' birth in Luke 1:29–33 confirm the covenant God made with David?

study

Look up Isaiah 9:1–7.

How was Jesus' reign as King prophesied long before His arrival?

In Mark 1:14–15, Jesus proclaims that the kingdom of God is near. His ministry is the beginning of the fulfillment of God's kingdom on earth, inviting people to repent and believe in the good news.

How does Jesus' proclamation in Mark 1:14–15 show that the kingdom of God is not just a future promise but a present reality?

Look up Matthew 4:17.

How does Jesus invite us to live in the reality of His kingdom today?

Jesus calls people to respond to the good news of the kingdom with repentance and belief. This is not just a call to turn away from sin but a call to live under the reign of Jesus as King.

What does it mean to repent and believe in the context of Jesus' kingdom?

How does this call challenge the way you live your life today?

Look up Colossians 1:13–14.

What do you think it means to be transferred from the kingdom of darkness to the kingdom of light?

reflect

Where in your life do you need to more fully submit to Jesus' reign? How can you live more faithfully as a citizen of His kingdom?

pray

Gracious and faithful God, I thank You for sending Jesus, the promised King, the fulfillment of every covenant and every promise You have made. His kingdom is eternal, and I am humbled to know that I am invited to live under His reign. Lord, help me to fully grasp what it means to live in Your kingdom today. Teach me to trust in Your sovereignty and goodness, even when life feels uncertain.

I ask for the grace to repent where I've strayed and to believe deeply in the good news that Your kingdom has come near. May my life reflect the hope, peace, and justice of Your kingdom, and may I always look to Jesus as my King. Strengthen my heart to live in the light of His reign and to walk in His ways.

In Jesus' name I pray, amen.

day 4

Thirsting for the Kingdom

In both the Old and New Testaments, the image of thirst is used to describe the deep longing for God and His kingdom. In Isaiah 55, the invitation is clear: all who are thirsty are welcome to come and drink freely from the waters of life. This is not just a physical thirst but a spiritual one—a longing for the presence of God and the fullness of His kingdom. In Revelation 22, this invitation is extended to the end of all things, where Jesus Himself calls us to drink from the waters of eternal life.

As we reflect on these passages, we're reminded that the kingdom of God is not just something we wait for—it's something we hunger and thirst for in our lives right now. God invites us to come, listen, and receive life. His kingdom is one where our deepest needs are met, and our thirst is quenched by the living water that Jesus offers.

read

Isaiah 55:1–3
Revelation 22:16–17

As we reflect on the invitation to come and drink from the waters of life, may we respond with open hearts, thirsting for God's kingdom and receiving His abundant grace. Let us find our satisfaction in Him, and may we invite others to experience the richness of life in His presence.

In both Isaiah and Revelation, there is a clear and open invitation to all who are thirsty to come and receive from God. This is not based on merit or wealth—it's a free gift to all who seek.

Why do you think God uses the image of thirst to describe our longing for Him and His kingdom?

study

Look up John 4:13–14.

How does Jesus fulfill this promise of living water?

Isaiah 55 speaks of the richness of what God offers—wine, milk, and the "richest of fare." This isn't just about physical sustenance but about the abundant, satisfying life that comes from being in relationship with God.

What does it mean to you that God offers to satisfy your deepest longings?

How do you experience this "richest of fare" in your relationship with Him?

Read Psalm 34:8 and prayerfully reflect on how God invites us to taste and see His goodness.

Record anything that stands out in your moment of prayer:

Isaiah 55:3 points back to the covenant God made with David, a promise of faithful love that will last forever. This covenant is ultimately fulfilled in Jesus, the "Root and Offspring of David" mentioned in Revelation 22:16.

How does the everlasting covenant with David tie into the invitation to drink from the waters of life?

Reread 2 Samuel 7:16 and reflect on the connection between God's promises to David and the fulfillment we know is in Jesus.

Make notes of the connections that stand out:

In Revelation 22, the invitation to come and drink is extended by both the Spirit and the bride, signifying the call of the church and the Spirit working together to invite all into God's kingdom.

How does this call to "come" in Revelation 22 reflect the heart of God's mission for the world?

How might you live out the invitation to come and drink in your own life as you invite others to experience the kingdom of God?

reflect

Reflect on the areas of your life where you feel spiritually thirsty. Consider how you might turn to God for true satisfaction.

pray

Spend a few moments in prayer, responding to what you've studied and reflected on. Here's a guide for your prayer:

- Thank God for the open invitation to come and drink from the water of life, for the ways He satisfies your deepest longings.
- Ask for the grace to thirst for His kingdom and to seek satisfaction in Him alone, trusting in His faithful love.
- Pray for the boldness to extend this invitation to others, sharing the life and hope found in Jesus with those around you.

The kingdom of God is not just something we wait for—it's something we hunger and thirst for in our lives right now.

day 5

guided contemplative prayer

read

Psalm 63:1–8

reflect

1. How does this psalm express a deep longing for God?
2. How does your own heart long for God in this season of your life?

guided prayer exercise

preparation

- Find a quiet space where you can be undisturbed.
- Take a few deep breaths to center yourself in God's presence.

meditation

- Slowly read Psalm 63:1–8 aloud, letting the words resonate in your heart.

reflection

- Reflect on how your soul thirsts for God and how He meets you in that longing.

breath prayer

- Breathe in: "O God, you are my God."
- Breathe out: "My soul thirsts for You."

closing prayer

- Thank God for satisfying your spiritual thirst and ask Him to continue drawing you closer to Him.

journaling

- On the next page, write a prayer of gratitude expressing your longing for God and your thankfulness for how He meets you in your thirst.

journaling prayer

Session 5

The Fulfillment of the Covenants in Jesus

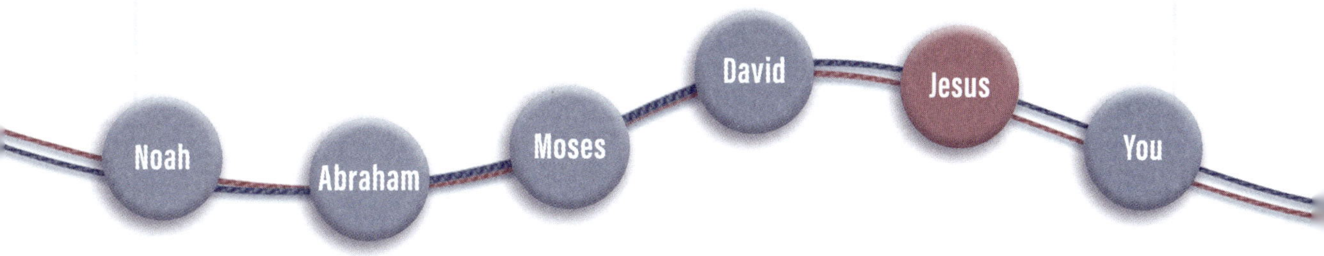

group session (90 minutes)

icebreaker and opening

Think about a time in your life when everything seemed to come together—when you had an "ah-ha" moment where you could see the bigger picture. What was that experience like?

opening reflection

Select a volunteer to read the following aloud to your group:

Over the past weeks, we've been threading together the story of God's covenants—His promises with Noah, Abraham, Moses, and David. Each of these covenants was a part of God's larger plan, a promise that He would be faithful, that He would dwell with His people, and that He would bring redemption. Today, we turn our eyes to Jesus, the One who doesn't just fulfill the covenants but threads them all together into something greater. Jesus is the living fulfillment of God's promises, the one who perfectly completes the covenant story and invites us into the kingdom of God.

As we dive into Matthew 5:17–20, we'll explore how Jesus fulfills the law and the prophets, threading together the old promises into a new reality. Let's open our hearts to the ways God has been weaving His story through the covenants, and how Jesus brings that story to its fullness.

prayer

Select a volunteer or pray together in unison:

> *Faithful God, we come before You with open hearts, ready to hear how Jesus is the fulfillment of Your promises. As we explore the teachings of Jesus, help us to see the thread of Your covenantal love and faithfulness woven through all of Scripture. Guide us to live as Your people, following Your ways and trusting in Your kingdom. Amen.*

read before watching

Ask a volunteer to read Matthew 5:17–20 aloud before watching the video.

In this passage, Jesus declares that He has come to fulfill the law and the prophets, not to abolish them, and He calls His followers to live out the commandments with even greater righteousness.

Today, we turn our eyes to Jesus, the One who doesn't just fulfill the covenants but threads them all together into something greater.

video

watch video session 5 (17 minutes)

The Fulfillment of the Covenants in Jesus

Leader, stream the video using access instructions on the inside front cover, or play the DVD (sold separately).

notes

Use this space to take notes from the teaching if you like.

group discussion

(40 minutes)

Leader, read the following prompts to the group for discussion.

Tara Beth unpacked how Jesus fulfills the covenants by threading together God's promises from the Old Testament into the kingdom reality we live in today. She explored how Jesus doesn't just replace the law but completes and perfects it, calling us to live in alignment with the heart of God's kingdom.

1. **Reflect on a time when you could clearly see God working through a long-standing promise in your life. How did that experience help you see the "bigger picture" of what God was doing? Share with the group.**

2. **In Matthew 5:17, Jesus says He came to fulfill the law and the prophets. What does it mean that Jesus is the fulfillment of the covenants? How does this understanding help you see the connection between the Old and New Testaments?**

3. **Have a volunteer read Luke 24:44 aloud to the group and make a list together of the ways in which you see God threading the entire story of Scripture together through Jesus.**

Jesus calls His followers to a deeper righteousness, one that goes beyond the mere external adherence to rules. The religious leaders of Jesus' time focused on the letter of the law, often missing the heart behind it. In Matthew 5:17–20, Jesus challenges this approach, saying that He came not to abolish the law but to fulfill it. This fulfillment isn't about discarding the law but embodying its true purpose—loving God and loving others. The deeper righteousness Jesus speaks of is about living in alignment with God's heart, where our thoughts, attitudes, and actions reflect His holiness and compassion. It's not just about outward behavior but also about transformation from the inside out. For us, this means we are called to live differently.

Jesus' fulfillment of the law empowers us to live in the freedom of God's grace, where we follow His ways not out of obligation but out of love. When we live in this deeper righteousness, we move beyond rule-keeping and legalism and instead seek to live by the Spirit. This type of righteousness means examining our hearts, being transformed by God's love, and allowing that transformation to shape how we treat others, how we forgive, and how we pursue justice. It's a call to reflect God's kingdom in every part of our lives, embodying His love and truth in the way we live and interact with the world.

Have another volunteer read Romans 8:3–4 aloud to the group.

4. Discuss practical and realistic ways we are called to walk by the Spirit in fulfilling God's law.

In the covenants we've studied, God's promises to dwell with His people, lead them, and bring redemption.

5. How does Jesus' life, death, and resurrection fulfill these covenant promises? In what ways does His kingdom reflect the heart of God's covenantal love?

Jesus invites us to live as citizens of His kingdom.

6. What does living as part of God's kingdom actually look like for you today?

7. How does seeing Jesus as the fulfillment of the covenants change the way you will live out your faith?

closing reflection

Leader, read these prompts to the group and provide some time for reflection and response.

- What is one key takeaway from today's discussion that you will carry with you this week?
- How can we pray for each other to live out the deeper righteousness that Jesus calls us to as citizens of God's kingdom?

close in prayer

Read aloud together or select a volunteer to pray over your group:

> *Dear and Gracious God, we thank You for threading together Your story of redemption through Jesus, the fulfillment of every covenant promise. Help us to live in the fullness of Your kingdom, walking in the deeper righteousness that Jesus calls us to. Empower us by Your Spirit to live as faithful followers, reflecting Your love and truth in all that we do. Amen.*

Jesus' fulfillment of the law empowers us to live in the freedom of God's grace.

Session 5

personal Bible study

The Fulfillment of the Covenants in Jesus

day 1

All Becomes Fulfilled

As we look again at Matthew 5:17–20, we'll dive deeper into Jesus' profound teaching about the law and the prophets. We've already seen how Jesus threads the covenants together, fulfilling the promises made to Noah, Abraham, Moses, and David. But now, Jesus challenges us to see that His fulfillment of the law is not the end of the story—it's an invitation into something deeper. Jesus invites us into a righteousness that transcends rule-keeping, weaving together God's heart for holiness and grace into a new way of living.

In this passage, Jesus reframes what it means to live in God's kingdom. He doesn't dismiss the law; instead, He perfects it by showing how it was always meant to lead to love—love for God and love for others. As we explore this passage in today's study, let's ask ourselves what it means to live in this deeper righteousness, where the law is not just a set of rules but an expression of God's grace and justice threaded through our lives.

read

Matthew 5:17–20

In this passage, Jesus invites us into a new way of understanding and living out the law, threading the heart of God's covenant with His people through His life and teaching.

study

Let's take a look at key themes:

Fulfilling, Not Abolishing, the Law

Jesus makes it clear that His mission was not to discard the law or the prophets but to fulfill them in ways the people had never fully understood. In fulfilling the law, Jesus is threading together the righteousness God has always intended for His people.

How does Jesus fulfill the law in a way that goes beyond mere rule-keeping?

Look up Romans 13:8–10.

How does love change the way we approach obedience?

Righteousness That Surpasses the Pharisees

Jesus calls His followers to a righteousness that surpasses the Pharisees and the teachers of the law, whose lives were focused on strict adherence to the letter of the law. But this deeper righteousness Jesus speaks of is about embodying the heart of the law—justice, mercy, and faithfulness—threading together outward action with inner transformation.

Consider what a Pharisee might be in your context today. What does it mean for your righteousness to surpass that of the Pharisees? (You may have a lot more in common with the Pharisees than you realize. It's okay! Jesus is about our transformation, not our performance.)

Look up Matthew 23:23–24. Jesus rebuked the Pharisees for missing the heart of the law.

How can you pursue justice, mercy, and faithfulness in your own life?

A New Way of Teaching and Living the Law

Jesus calls us not only to practice the commands of God but also to teach them. But what we are called to practice and teach isn't legalism—it's a deeper way of life that reflects the kingdom of God, where grace, love, and justice are threaded together in perfect harmony.

How might we both practice and teach this deeper righteousness? Make a list that is practical, actionable, clear, and realistic. Commit to putting this list into action and check in with yourself in the coming weeks to maintain your commitment.

reflect

Jesus calls us to live out a righteousness that is deeper than simply following rules. What does it look like for you to live in this deeper righteousness, where the law is threaded with love, justice, and grace? How can you begin to teach and model this way of life to others?

pray

Spend time in prayer, asking God to help you live out this deeper righteousness. Here's a guide for your prayer:

- Thank God for sending Jesus to fulfill the law and for inviting you into a new way of living in the kingdom.

- Ask for the grace to live in the deeper righteousness that surpasses legalism, embodying the heart of the law in your actions and attitudes.
- Pray for the wisdom to teach and model this way of life to others, threading God's love, justice, and grace through everything you do.

Jesus calls us not only to practice the commands of God but also to teach them.

day 2

Jesus, the Light of the World

From the very beginning, God has made covenants with His people, promising life, blessing, and restoration. The covenant with Abraham promised that through his offspring, all nations would be blessed (Genesis 12:1–3). The Mosaic Covenant established a path of righteousness and holiness, and the Davidic Covenant pointed toward an eternal kingdom. Each of these promises pointed toward a future hope—a future light.

Jesus, as the light of the world, is the ultimate fulfillment of these covenant promises. In Him the blessings of Abraham extend to all nations. In Him the law of Moses is fulfilled through perfect righteousness. In Him the eternal kingdom of David is established. Jesus doesn't just bring light; He is the light that shines into the darkness of our world, fulfilling God's promises and inviting us to walk in that light. Today, let's explore how Jesus' identity as the light of the world is deeply rooted in God's covenant promises.

read

John 1:4–5

study

Let's take a deeper look at how Jesus, as the light of the world, fulfills the covenant promises:

Jesus and the Abrahamic Covenant

With the covenant given to Abraham, God promised that through his descendants, all nations would be blessed. Jesus, as the light of the world, extends God's blessing to all people, bringing salvation to every tribe, tongue, and nation.

Make a list of as many ways as you can describing how Jesus fulfills God's promise to bless all nations through Abraham:

Look up Galatians 3:8–9.

What do these verses mean to you as Gentile believer or perhaps someone considering faith in Jesus Christ?

Jesus and the Mosaic Covenant

The law given to Moses provided a guide for how God's people should live in righteousness, but no one could fully keep it. Jesus, as the light, perfectly fulfills the law, shining in the darkness of our sin and bringing life through His obedience.

Look up Matthew 5:17–20.

In what ways does Jesus fulfill the law beyond mere rule-keeping?

How does this relate to His role as the light of the world?

Jesus and the Davidic Covenant

The covenant with David promised an eternal kingdom through his lineage. Jesus, the light that cannot be overcome by darkness, establishes this kingdom through His death and resurrection, securing an eternal reign of righteousness.

Read Isaiah 53–55.

Describe how Jesus secures the everlasting kingdom promised to David.

reflect

Jesus' light is not just a source of guidance or comfort; it's the fulfillment of centuries of covenant promises made by God to His people. As you think about Jesus' role as the fulfillment of these covenants, where do you see His light breaking through the darkness in your life?

What does it mean for you to walk in the light of His fulfilled promises?

pray

Dear Gracious and Faithful God,

We come before You in awe of the way You have woven Your promises through history, all finding their fulfillment in Jesus, the Light of the World. Thank You for the gift of life that shines through the darkness, for the hope that cannot be extinguished, and for the love that meets us right where we are.

Lord, we are humbled by the way Your covenant promises reach us today. In our doubts, struggles, and joys Your light never fades. Help us to walk in that light, to trust in Your promises, and to be a people who reflect the love and grace You have so freely given to us.

Father, we ask for the courage to live in the fullness of Your light. May we be a community that radiates Your love to the world, living out the covenant of grace and truth You have made with us through Jesus. And for those who feel lost in darkness, may Your light find them, bringing healing, hope, and peace.

We offer all this to You, trusting in Your faithfulness. In the name of Jesus, the fulfillment of all Your promises, we pray. Amen.

day 3

The New Covenant in Jesus' Blood

As we come to this pivotal moment in Luke's Gospel, we find Jesus with His disciples at the Last Supper. This was the traditional Passover meal celebrated every year by the Jews, but Jesus reframes it, revealing that something new was unfolding—the promise of a new covenant sealed not with the blood of a lamb but with His own blood. The disciples were no strangers to the idea of covenant, which was rooted in their history and faith, but Jesus now reveals that the ultimate covenant is about to be fulfilled.

This new covenant is not written on stone tablets but on the hearts of all who follow Him. It is a covenant of grace, sealed by the sacrificial love of Jesus, offering us forgiveness and reconciliation with God. Today, we will explore what it means to live under this new covenant and how the blood of Jesus invites us into a life of freedom, forgiveness, and transformation.

read

Luke 22:14–20

study

In Luke 22:20, Jesus speaks of the cup as "the new covenant in my blood." This statement would have been startling to the disciples, who were celebrating the Passover and remembering God's deliverance of Israel from Egypt. Now, Jesus is saying that His blood, like the blood of the Passover lamb, would be poured out for their deliverance.

What do you think it means that Jesus' blood is the foundation of this new covenant?

Look up Exodus 24:8.

How does Jesus' new covenant compare to the old one?

In the early covenants, it was required for sacrifices to be offered regularly to atone for sin. But now, Jesus' sacrifice is once and for all, offering full forgiveness and reconciliation with God. His blood represents not just the forgiveness of sins, but the transformation of our hearts and lives.

How does the new covenant differ from the ones that came before it?

How does it invite us into an ever-deepening relationship with God?

Look up Jeremiah 31:31–34.

How does this passage prepare the way for the new covenant in Jesus' blood?

Jesus instructs His disciples to remember Him whenever they eat the bread and drink the cup. This act of remembrance is not just about recalling the events of the Last Supper—it's a reminder of the new life we've been given through the sacrifice of Jesus.

How does participating in communion deepen your understanding of Jesus' sacrifice and help you live in the reality of the grace He offers through the new covenant?

reflect

The new covenant in Jesus' blood offers us forgiveness and new life. As you reflect on today's passage, think about how this covenant shapes your relationship with God and others. How does the reality of Jesus' sacrifice change the way you live each day?

Where is God inviting you to live more fully in the grace and freedom of this new covenant?

pray

Spend time in prayer, thanking Jesus for the gift of the new covenant sealed in His blood. Here's a guide for your prayer:

- Thank God for the new covenant, where grace and forgiveness flow freely through Jesus' sacrifice.
- Ask for the strength to live in the fullness of this new covenant, embracing the freedom and transformation it brings.
- Pray for a deeper understanding of what it means to be in covenant with God, trusting in His faithfulness and love.

day 4

Living as Citizens of the Kingdom

At the very beginning of Jesus' ministry, He announces something radical: the kingdom of God is at hand. It's not a distant promise or something only to hope for in the future; it is here right now, breaking into the world through Jesus Himself. His proclamation invites a response—repentance and belief in the good news.

Living as citizens of God's kingdom means more than just acknowledging the reign of God; it's about aligning our lives with His purposes, turning away from old patterns, and embracing a new way of life rooted in His grace and truth. Today, we'll explore what it means to live as citizens of this kingdom that has come near, and how Jesus' invitation to repent and believe transforms the way we live in the world.

read

Mark 1:14–15

When Jesus began His public ministry, His first words were a declaration of the kingdom of God. This was the long-awaited hope of Israel—that God would reign as King and bring about justice, peace, and restoration. Yet Jesus' announcement wasn't just about a future kingdom but rather one that was breaking into the world now through His very presence

study

Jesus' proclamation that "the kingdom of God has come near" was revolutionary. For centuries, Israel had been waiting for the Messiah who would establish God's reign on earth. Yet Jesus wasn't announcing an earthly political kingdom—He was speaking about God's reign breaking into human history in a new and profound way. The kingdom wasn't just a distant hope; it was being realized in the present.

What does it mean that the kingdom of God is not just a future reality but has already come near through Jesus?

Read and fill in the chart:

Read	Write the Prophecy	Fulfillment in Jesus
Daniel 2:44		
Isaiah 9:6–7		

Consider how the kingdom of God challenges the values of the world. Make a list of comparisons below:

Values of Earthly Kingdoms	Values of God's Kingdom

Record your definition of the word *repentance*:

Repentance in Jesus' day was often associated with turning from sin, but it's more than just personal behavior change. The Greek word for repentance, *metanoia*, means "a change of mind" or "a new way of thinking." Jesus was calling people to rethink their understanding of God's kingdom, to turn away from their old allegiances and embrace the new reality He was bringing.

How does this understanding of repentance challenge you?

Make a list of areas of your life where you need a "change of mind" to align with the kingdom of God:

Look up Romans 12:1–8.

How do these verses change or alter your understanding of what it is to live as citizens of God's kingdom?

What are some areas you can seek God's help to grow more reflective of kingdom citizenship?

In the Gospel of Mark, Jesus says, "The time has come, and God's kingdom is near. Change the way you think and act, and believe the Good News" (Mark 1:15).

What is the good news of the kingdom, and how does it differ from the messages we hear from the world?

Read and fill in the chart:

Describe the good news of the kingdom in Jesus Christ.	Describe the different messages of what is "good" we hear from the world.

The kingdom of God has come near, but we also know that the fullness of the kingdom is still to come when Jesus returns. We live in the tension of the "already and not yet"—where God's reign has begun but is not yet fully realized. This tension calls us to live in hope and anticipation, working for God's justice and peace while also waiting for His ultimate restoration.

In what ways do you experience the "already and not yet" of the kingdom in your life?

In what ways have you seen glimpses of God's reign, and in what ways do you still long for His kingdom to come fully?

Read Revelation 21–22. How does this vision give you hope and shape the way you live today?

To live as a citizen of the kingdom means that we live under the authority of Jesus as our King. It means that our allegiance is to Him above all else, and our lives should reflect the values of the kingdom—justice, mercy, love, and humility.

In what real and practical ways does living under the rule of Jesus change the way you interact with the world, with your community, and with those who do not yet know Christ?

reflect

As you reflect on today's passage and study, think about the ways in which you are called to live as a citizen of God's kingdom. Where in your life do you need to repent and realign with the values of the kingdom?

What does it look like for you to live in the "already and not yet" tension of God's reign?

pray

Spend time in prayer, asking God to help you live as a citizen of His kingdom, trusting in the good news of Jesus. Here's a guide for your prayer:

- Thank God for the gift of His kingdom, which has come near through Jesus, and for the hope of its future fulfillment.
- Ask for the grace to repent and realign your life with the values of the kingdom, seeking justice, mercy, and humility in all that you do.
- Pray for the strength to live faithfully as a citizen of God's kingdom in the tension of the "already and not yet," trusting in His promises and working for His purposes in the world.

day 5

guided contemplative prayer

read

Psalm 46:1–11

reflect

1. How does this psalm encourage you to trust in God's strength and refuge?
2. What does it mean for God to be "our refuge and strength, an ever-present help in trouble"?

guided prayer exercise

preparation

- Find a quiet space where you can focus on God's presence.
- Take a few deep breaths to center yourself in His peace.

meditation

- Slowly read Psalm 46:1–11 aloud, letting the words resonate in your heart.

reflection

- Reflect on how God has been a refuge and strength for you in the past.

breath prayer

- Breathe in: "God, You are my refuge."
- Breathe out: "I trust in You."

closing prayer

- Thank God for being your ever-present help in times of trouble and ask Him to strengthen your trust in Him.

journaling

- On the next page, write a prayer of trust, expressing your confidence in God's protection and guidance.

journaling prayer

Session 6

Threaded Together

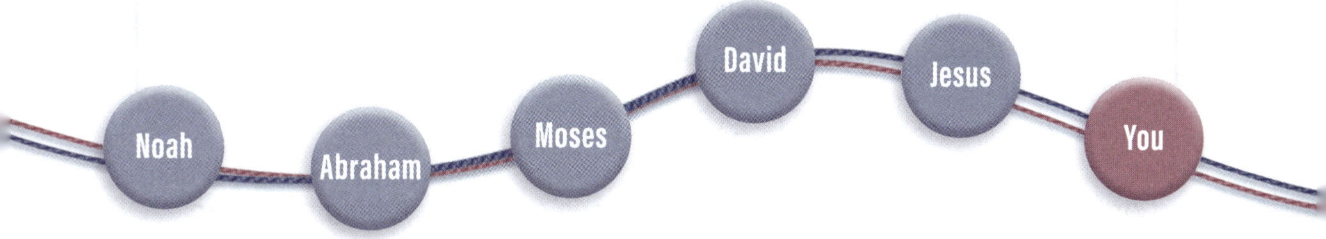

group session (90 minutes)

icebreaker and opening

Think of a time when you felt like your life was going in the wrong direction. How did God meet you in that season and redirect you?

opening reflection

Select a volunteer to read the following aloud to your group:

For the last five weeks, we've journeyed through the covenants of God and seen how, through twists and turns, nothing is wasted in God's kingdom. We've seen that being God's covenant people doesn't mean life will follow our perfect plan, but it means that in every twist, God is faithful to His promises.

In today's session, we will reflect on what it means to live as covenant people, not in a life of perfection or control but in a life marked by faithfulness, trust, and a deep understanding that nothing in our journey is ever wasted. Together, we'll explore how God's redemption threads through our stories, even when it feels like we're going in the wrong direction.

prayer

Select a volunteer or pray together in unison:

> *Father, we thank You for Your unending faithfulness. As we reflect on what it means to live as Your covenant people, may we see Your hand in every twist and turn of our lives. Open our hearts to trust Your direction, even when we don't understand it, and to live with the confidence that nothing is wasted in Your kingdom. Amen.*

read before watching

Ask a volunteer to read Romans 8:28 aloud before watching the video.

video

watch video session 6 (21:30 minutes)
Threaded Together

Leader, stream the video using access instructions on the inside front cover, or play the DVD (sold separately).

notes

Use this space to take notes from the teaching if you like.

group discussion

(40 minutes)

Leader, read the following prompts to the group for discussion.

1. **Have you ever had a season in life where you felt like everything was going backward or falling apart? How did you see God at work in that season?**

Select a volunteer to read God's message to His people in Isaiah 43:18–19 aloud to the group.

2. **How does this passage challenge us to trust in God's direction, even when we feel like we are lost or going the wrong way?**

Tara Beth mentioned that the Israelites often grumbled in the wilderness. How do you respond when life takes a detour? Do you trust God's plan, or do you, like the Israelites, find yourself grumbling?

Have another volunteer read Exodus 16:2–3 to the group.

3. **How does the Israelites' response in the wilderness mirror our own reactions to detours and delays? How can we cultivate a heart of trust rather than frustration?**

4. **Reflect on your personal journey. Can you identify moments where you now see that God was weaving His redemptive thread even in the hard times? Share an example.**

5. **What does it mean for God's people to wait well?**

6. **How can we learn from the waiting periods in Scripture? (For example, Abraham waiting for a son, the Israelites waiting for deliverance.)**

7. **How does living as a covenant people in the "already but not yet" world impact the way you approach challenges, suffering, and disappointments?**

Philippians 1:6 (ESV) says, "I am sure of this, that he who began a good work in you will bring it to completion at the day of Jesus Christ."

Read this aloud for the group:

> As we conclude this study, we stand at the culmination of a journey that has woven through the pages of Scripture, from God's covenant with Noah through the promises to Abraham, the giving of the law to Moses, the establishment of David's eternal throne, and the fulfillment of it all in Jesus Christ. We've seen that life is filled with twists and turns, and yet, through every detour, every season of waiting, every moment of suffering, God is at work, never wasting a single ounce of our lives.
>
> We are covenant people—living in the tension of the already and the not yet—trusting in the promise that God's redemption story is being written in each of us. The threads of God's faithfulness, power, and grace are not abstract ideas; they are woven into our very being, shaping us to be a people of hope, resilience, and trust. As we move forward from this final session, the challenge is not simply to remember what we've learned but to embody it.
>
> We are called to live as covenant people every single day—people who trust in God's promises, who reflect His grace and mercy, and who walk in faith even when the way seems unclear. Just as God has been faithful throughout history, He is faithful now and will continue to be as we step into whatever is next.
>
> So, the challenge is this: How will you live differently because of this journey? How will you allow God's covenant promises

to shape your identity, relationships, and purpose? May you walk forward, not with a sense of closure, but with an anticipation of the ongoing story God is writing in and through you. This is not the end; it's the beginning of a new chapter in living as His covenant people. Let's embrace the journey ahead with bold faith, knowing that nothing is wasted, and everything is held in the hands of our redeeming God.

closing reflection

Leader, read these prompts to the group and provide some time for reflection and response.

- What is one truth you will take with you from this group discussion as you seek to live as part of God's covenant people?
- How can we pray for each other as we live in the already but not yet, trusting that God is using every moment for His purposes?

close in prayer

Read aloud together or select a volunteer to pray over the group:

Heavenly Father, thank You for Your faithfulness, even in the moments we don't understand. We trust that nothing in our lives is wasted, and that You are weaving a thread of redemption through every twist and turn. Help us to live as Your covenant people, trusting in Your promises and following Your lead, no matter where You take us. In Jesus' name, amen.

Leader, offer this closing benediction to your group. Invite your group to open their hands in the posture of receiving, and extend your hands to your group in the posture of giving:

Beloved, as we go from this place, let us remember that we are a covenant people—called, chosen, and dearly loved by the God who writes our stories with His faithfulness. May you walk in the assurance that no twist, no turn, no valley of suffering, no moment of doubt is ever wasted in the hands of our Redeemer. Our God, the same God who called Abraham, who parted the Red Sea, who gave us Jesus—the fulfillment of every promise—is with you. He is for you. And He will never leave you or forsake you.

So go and live boldly in the truth of His covenant love. Step into the unknown with faith, knowing that the God who has begun a good work in you will see it to completion. Let His grace pour over every part of your life—shaping you, molding you, and making you a beacon of His light and love in this world.

And now, may the Lord bless you and keep you. May the Lord make His face shine upon you and be gracious to you. May the Lord lift up His countenance upon you and give you peace, now and forevermore. In the name of Jesus, the one who was, and is, and is to come—the King of Kings and the Lord of Lords, and the One who threads every promise with His eternal love—go in peace, go in courage, go in the power of the Holy Spirit. Amen and amen!

Go and live boldly in the truth of His covenant love.

the thread continues

As we draw this study to a close, take a deep breath and reflect on the journey you've been on over the last several weeks. It's a journey that has taken us through the deep, rich soil of God's covenants—each one revealing more of His character, His heart for redemption, and His unshakable plan to restore what was once broken. From the earliest moments in Genesis, when God promised never to flood the earth again, to the new covenant sealed in the blood of Jesus Christ, these covenants are not isolated promises but are woven threads of a single tapestry that display God's faithfulness throughout redemptive history.

Throughout this study, we've traced a redemptive thread, a theme that ties each covenant together and invites us to trust that God is working a plan far greater than we can comprehend. It's a plan that was never derailed by humanity's sin or by the brokenness of the world. God's promise was never just about a return to the way things were; it has always been about something even better—a renewed creation, a new heavens and a new earth, where God's *shalom* will reign eternally. This is the story we are part of today.

the faithfulness of God in every covenant

When we began with the Noahic Covenant, we encountered a God who, after a catastrophic flood, promised to never destroy the earth in that way again. The sign of the rainbow became a lasting reminder that God is committed to preserving life, even when humanity fails to uphold its part of the relationship. In this covenant, we saw God's mercy extended not only to Noah but to all of creation. It reminds us that despite the chaos we see in the world, God's ultimate aim is restoration, not destruction. We can trust Him to uphold life, even when all seems lost.

From there, we moved into the **Abrahamic Covenant**, where God chose one man and his descendants to be the people through whom all the nations of the world would be blessed. Abraham's faith and obedience became a model for us—an invitation to trust God even when we can't see how His promises will unfold. Through Abraham, God made a covenant not just with an individual but with a family that would grow into a nation and eventually bring forth the Savior of the world. This covenant shows us that God's plan is always unfolding, even when it seems slow. His promises are worth the wait, because they are deeply tied to His faithfulness.

The **Mosaic Covenant** took us to a mountaintop, where God gave His people the law—a framework for living in right relationship with Him and with each other. Through the Ten Commandments and the rest of the law, we learned that God's covenants are not just about promises but also about partnership. He invites us to participate in His work of restoration by living according to His ways. The law revealed both the heart of God—His desire for justice, mercy, and love—and the brokenness of humanity, unable to fully live up to it. Yet, even here God's grace is woven through. The Mosaic Covenant pointed forward to the ultimate fulfillment of the law in Jesus Christ, who would perfectly embody all that God desires for humanity.

In the **Davidic Covenant**, we saw God's promise to establish the kingdom of God through David that would last forever. Though David was a flawed man, God chose him to be the ancestor of the Messiah, the true King who would reign with justice and righteousness. This covenant reminds us that God's purposes are never thwarted by human imperfection. Even in our weakness, God's strength is made perfect, and His plan continues to unfold.

Finally, we reached the **new covenant**, which was inaugurated by Jesus, sealed in His blood, and has been made available to all who believe. Here, we saw the ultimate fulfillment of every promise that came before. Jesus is the fulfillment of the law, the Seed of Abraham, the King in David's line, and the One who brings *shalom* to the world. In this new covenant, we find forgiveness, reconciliation, and the promise of eternal life. It is the covenant that draws us into the heart of God's plan for redemption—not just for Israel, but for all people, for all time.

trusting the plan

As we reflect on the entire scope of these covenants, one thing becomes clear: God has always had a plan. It's a plan that was established before the foundations of the world, a plan to restore and renew all of creation. Even when things seem to go off course, even when sin and brokenness enter the picture, God's plan remains firm. The covenants we've studied are sure and steady reminders that God's promises are trustworthy and true.

But perhaps the most beautiful aspect of God's plan is that *it includes us*. You and I are part of this story. Through Jesus, we have been grafted into the family of God. We are participants in this new covenant who have been called to live out the reality of God's promises in our everyday lives. The covenants remind us that we are not passive recipients of God's grace but active participants in His redemptive work. We are called to embody the love, justice, and mercy of God in a world that is still longing for redemption.

contemplative prayer: living into the mystery

Throughout this study, we've also practiced the ancient discipline of **contemplative prayer**. This practice has allowed us to quiet our hearts, still our minds, and rest in the presence of God. Contemplative prayer invites us into the mystery of God's presence, teaching us to listen more than we speak and to rest more than we strive. It reminds us, as Teresa of Avila said, "Prayer is nothing else than being on terms of friendship with God." In these moments of quiet, we've learned that God is always near, always weaving the threads of redemption in our lives, even when we can't see it.

As we leave this study, let us carry the practice of contemplative prayer with us. It is a practice that roots us in the reality of God's presence even in the midst of the busyness of life. Let it remind us that God's plan is always unfolding, even when we can't see it, and that His faithfulness is as sure as the rising sun.

the story continues

While this study comes to a close, the story of God's redemptive plan does not. We are still living in the tension of the already and the not yet—the reality that Jesus has inaugurated the new covenant, but we have not yet seen its full consummation. As we await the return of Christ and the renewal of all things, we are called to live as **covenant people**, trusting in God's promises and partnering with Him in His work of redemption.

So, what now? How will you carry the truths of this study forward into your life? How will you live as a faithful participant in the story of God's covenants? My prayer for you is that you would continue to trust in the thread of God's faithfulness, knowing that even when the world seems broken, even when your life feels unraveled, God is still at work. His promises are sure. His love is steadfast. And His plan is unfolding, one thread at a time.

May you go forth with confidence, knowing that the God who made a covenant with Noah, who called Abraham, who gave the law to Moses, who established a kingdom through David, and who sealed the new covenant through Jesus Christ—this same God is with you, weaving the threads of redemption in your life and in the world around you.

Go in peace, to love and serve the Lord. Amen.

leader's guide

If you are reading this, you have likely agreed to lead group through *Threaded: Unraveling Our Story Through God's Covenants*. Thank you! What you have chosen to do is important, and much good fruit can come from studies like this. The rewards of being a leader are different from those of participating, and we hope you find your own walk with Jesus deepened by this experience.

Threaded is a six-session study built around video teaching content and small-group interaction. As the group leader, imagine yourself as the host of a dinner party without dinner, unless of course that's your thing. Your job is to take care of your "guests" so that as they arrive, they feel comfortable and welcomed and excited to learn straight away.

As the group leader, you are more of a facilitator than a teacher. Your role is NOT to answer all the questions or reteach the content—I, Tara Beth, am the teacher on video and the study guide will prompt how the group experience will flow. Your job is to guide the experience and cultivate your small group into a learning and growing community. This will make it a place for members to process, question, reflect, and grow *together*.

There are several elements in this leader's guide that will help you as you structure your study and reflection time, so follow along and take advantage of each one.

before you begin

materials

Before your first meeting, make sure the participants have a copy of this study guide. Alternately, you can hand out the study guides at your first meeting and give the group members some time to look over the material and ask any preliminary questions. During your first meeting, be sure to send a sheet around the room and have the members write down their name, phone number, and email address so you can keep in touch with them during the week.

free streaming video access

Additionally, spend a few minutes going over how to access the FREE streaming video using the code printed on the inside front cover of each study guide. Helping everyone understand how accessible this material is will go a long way if anyone (including you) has to miss a meeting or if any member of your group chooses to lead a study after the conclusion of this one!

A few commonly asked questions and answers:

Do I have to subscribe to StudyGateway? NO. If you sign up for StudyGateway for the first time using: **studygateway.com/redeem** you will *not* be prompted to subscribe, then or after.

Do I set up another account if I do another study later? NO. The next time you do a HarperChristian Resources study with FREE streaming access, all you need to do is enter the new access code and the videos will be added to your account library.

There is a short video available walking through how to access your streaming videos. You can choose to show the video at your first meeting, or simply direct your group to the HarperChristian Resources YouTube channel to watch it at their convenience.

HOW TO ACCESS FREE STEAMING VIDEOS:
https://youtu.be/JPhG06ksOn8

group size

Generally, the ideal size for a group is between eight to ten people, which ensures everyone will have enough time to participate in discussions. If you have more people, you might want to break up the main group into smaller subgroups. Encourage those who show up at the first meeting to commit to attending the duration of the study, as this will help the group members get to know each other, create stability for the group, and help you know how to prepare each week.

opening

Each of the sessions begins with an opening ice breaker question, a contextual passage to set the stage for each week's teaching, a prayer, and a portion of Scripture that will be the focus of the teaching to read as a group.

Whenever prompted to select a volunteer to read a passage of any sort, please take the temperature of the room, as it were. Note the members of your group who do not readily raise their hand to volunteer. Reading Scripture aloud can incite anxiety or nervousness in some people. Please take the time in Session One to communicate the value of reading Scripture aloud as a community, in community. Encourage all your group members to try it at some point. Be clear that there is no bad reading of God's Word, rather it is *meant* to be read and shared with others. So, consider your group space a safe place to try and grow in this practice. One goal of this study is to grow participants in their overall engagement of God's Word which includes feeling comfortable and confident with the words on the pages!

preparing your group for the study

Before watching your first video at your first meeting, let the group members know that each session contains four days' worth of Bible study and reflection materials to complete during the week between group meetings. While the personal study is optional, it will help the members cement the concepts presented during the group study time and encourage them to spend time each day in God's Word. One of the most lamented aspects of all church ministry is struggling to get people to read their Bible on their own. It is my prayer and hope that you and your group will find joy and anticipation in reading God's Word afresh during this study.

Also, invite your group members to bring any questions and insights they uncovered while reading to your next meeting, especially if they had a breakthrough moment or if they didn't understand something.

weekly preparation

As the leader, there are a few things you should do to prepare for each meeting:

- ***Watch the video.*** This will help you to become familiar with the content I am presenting and give you foresight of what may or may not be brought up in the discussion time.
- ***Read through the group discussion section.*** This will help you to become familiar with the questions you will be asking, the focus Scripture, and the context. This practice allows you to better anticipate any alterations you might need or want to make in the discussion time for your best group experience.
- ***Decide which questions you definitely want to discuss.*** Based on the amount and length of group discussion, you may not be able to get through all the questions, so choose four to five questions that you *definitely* want to cover.
- ***Be familiar with the questions you want to discuss.*** Every group has times when there are no respondents and the question falls flat out of the gate. This is normal and okay! Be prepared with YOUR answer to the questions so you can always offer to share as an icebreaker and example. **What you want to avoid is always answering the questions and therefore speaking for the group.** Foremost encourage members of the group to answer questions.
- ***Remind your group there are no wrong answers or dumb questions.*** Note that in many cases there will not be one "right" answer to the question. Answers will vary, especially when the group members are being asked to share their personal experiences.
- ***Pray for your group.*** Pray for your group members throughout the week and ask God to lead them as they study His Word.
- ***Bring extra supplies to your meeting.*** The members should bring their own pens for writing notes, but it's a good idea to have extras available for those who forget. You may also want to bring paper and additional

Bibles. If you find group members who are without a personal copy of the Bible, please let me know. There are a lot of great resources for low-cost outreach Bibles. I do not want anyone to be without a copy of the Bible if I can help it!

structuring the discussion time

You will need to determine with your group how long you want to meet each week so you can plan your time accordingly. Generally, most groups like to meet for either sixty minutes or ninety minutes, so you could use one of the following schedules:

Section	60 minutes	90 minutes
Introduction (members arrive and get settled; leader reads or summarizes introduction)	2 minutes	2 minutes
Opening Activity	10 minutes	10 minutes
Video Notes (watch the teaching video together and take notes)	20 minutes	20 minutes
Group Discussion (discuss the Bible study questions you selected ahead of time)	25 minutes	55 minutes
Closing Prayer (pray together as a group and dismiss)	3 minutes	3 minutes

As the group leader, it is up to you to keep track of the time and keep things moving along according to your schedule. You might want to set a timer for each segment so both you and the group members know when your time is up. (Note that there are some good phone apps for timers that play a gentle chime or other pleasant sound instead of a disruptive noise.)

Don't be concerned if the group members are quiet or slow to share. People are often quiet when they are pulling together their ideas, and this might be a new experience for them. Just ask a question and let it hang in the air until someone shares. You can then say, "Thank you. What about others? What came to you when you watched that portion of the video?"

group dynamics

Leading a group through *Threaded* will prove to be highly rewarding both to you and your group members. However, this doesn't mean you will not encounter any challenges along the way! Discussions can get off track. Group members may not be sensitive to the needs and ideas of others. Some might worry they will be expected to talk about matters that make them feel awkward. Others may express comments that result in disagreements. To help ease this strain on you and the group, consider the following ground rules:

- When someone raises a question or comment that is off the main topic, suggest you deal with it another time, or, if you feel led to go in that direction, let the group know you will be spending some time discussing it.
- If someone asks a question you don't know how to answer, admit it and move on. At your discretion, feel free to invite group members to comment on questions that call for personal experience.
- If you find one or two people are dominating the discussion time, direct a few questions to others in the group. Outside the main group time, ask the more dominating members to help you draw out the quieter ones. Work to make them a part of the solution instead of the problem.
- When a disagreement occurs, encourage the group members to process the matter *in love*. Encourage those on opposite sides to restate what they heard the other side say about the matter, and then invite each side to evaluate if that perception is accurate. Lead the group in examining other Scriptures related to the topic and look for common ground.

When any of these issues arise, encourage your group members to follow these words from the Bible: "Love one another" (John 13:34), "If it is possible, as far as it depends on you, live at peace with everyone" (Romans 12:18), and "Be quick to listen, slow to speak and slow to become angry" (James 1:19). This will make your group time more rewarding and beneficial for everyone who attends.

session by session overviews

session one: The Covenant With Noah

Scripture covered in this session**: Genesis 6–9**

Scripture to study and read this week: **Genesis 6; 7:1-5; John 12:50; Hebrews 11:7; Genesis 7; Genesis 8; Genesis 1:26-31; Genesis 9; Psalm 136:1-9**

Discussion Question choices / notes:

Prayer requests

session two: The Covenant with Abraham

Scripture covered in this session: **Genesis 12:1–4; 15:1–6; Hebrews 11:8-1; Galatians 3:7–9**

Scripture to study and read this week: **Genesis 12:1–9; Genesis 15: 1–6; Galatians 3:7–9; Genesis 16:1–4; Genesis 17:1–8; Proverbs 3:5–6; Isaiah 40:28–31; 2 Corinthians 5:17; Deuteronomy 30:6; Galatians 3:28–30; Romans 4:13–25; Psalm 105:1–11**

Discussion Question choices / notes:

Prayer requests

session three: The Covenant with Moses

Scripture covered in this session: **Exodus 19:3–6; 20:1–17; Romans 8:1–4**

Scripture to read this week: **Exodus 19:1–6; Deuteronomy 7:6–8; 1 Peter 2:9–10; John 15:9–11; Exodus 20:1–7; Exodus 19:4–6; Matthew 22:34–40; Hebrews 13:15–16; Psalm 96:1–3; Exodus 24:1–8; Deuteronomy 30:19–20; Hebrews 9:19–22; James 1:22–25; Psalm 119:33–40**

Discussion Question choices / notes:

Prayer requests

session four: The Covenant with David

Scripture covered in this session: **2 Samuel 7:8–16; Luke 1:29–33; Acts 13:21–23**

Scripture to study and read this week: **2 Samuel 7:1-17; Isaiah 55:8-9; Hebrews 12:5-6; Isaiah 9:1-7; Jeremiah 23:5-6; Luke 1:29-33; Philippians 1:6; Matthew 6:33; Mark 1:14-15, Matthew 4:17; Colossians 1:13-14; Isaiah 55:1-3; Revelation 22:16-17; John 4:13-14; Psalm 34:8; Psalm 63:1-8**

Discussion Question choices / notes:

Prayer requests

session five: The Fulfillment of the Covenants in Jesus

Scripture covered in this session: **Matthew 5:17–20; Luke 24:44; Romans 8:3–4**

Scripture to study and read this week: **Matthew 5:17-20; Romans 13:8-10; Matthew 22:23-24; John 1:4-5; Galatians 3:8-9; Matthew 5:17-20; Isaiah 53-55; Luke 22:14-20; Exodus 24:8; Jeremiah 31:31-34; Mark 1:14-15; Daniel 2:44; Isaiah 9:6-7; Romans 12:1-8; Psalm 46:1-11**

Discussion Question choices / notes:

Prayer requests

session six: Threaded Together

Scripture covered in this session: **Romans 8:28; Isaiah 43:18–19; Exodus 16:2–3**

There is no personal homework this week as you wrap your study. Please make plans for some form of celebration or acknowledgment of the completion of this study together and how you have grown as a group of believers in your faith. There is additional content to share after the group discussion section this week: *The Thread Continues*. I encourage you to read it and discern if you want to read it together as a group or simply direct your group members to read it on their own this coming week.

Discussion Question choices / notes:

Prayer requests

about the author

Tara Beth Leach is a pastor, preacher of the Word, and writer. She speaks widely at conferences, retreats, and universities across the country on Women in Ministry, Church Leadership, and the call to be a Radiant Witness. She is the Senior Pastor at Good Shepherd Church in Naperville, IL and previously served at Christ Church in Oakbrook and as Senior Pastor of First Church of the Nazarene of Pasadena ("PazNaz") in SoCal. She is a graduate of Olivet Nazarene University and Northern Theological Seminary and has authored three books, including Emboldened and Radiant Church. Tara Beth is the co-founder of Propel Ecclesia and is also the co-host of The Pastors Table podcast. She has two beautiful and rambunctious sons and has been married to the love of her life, Jeff, since 2006.

From the Publisher

GREAT STUDIES

ARE EVEN BETTER WHEN THEY'RE SHARED!

Help others find this study:

- Post a review at your favorite online bookseller.
- Post a picture on a social media account and share why you enjoyed it.
- Send a note to a friend who would also love it—or, better yet, go through it with them.

Thanks for helping others grow their faith!